Child of the Theatre

Elizabeth Brunner in her forties

Child of the Theatre

Elizabeth Brunner

With an afterword by
Hugo Brunner

THE PERPETUA PRESS
OXFORD

For Violet Miller, née Bentley
dear friend of Elizabeth and Hugo

First published in Great Britain 2010
by The Perpetua Press
26 Norham Road, Oxford OX2 6SF

Reprinted with minor corrections,
additional photographs and a new cover 2016

ISBN 978 1 870882 25 5

Designed and typeset in Monotype Bembo
by The Stonesfield Press, Stonesfield, Witney, Oxon

Printed and bound in Great Britain
by Holywell Press Ltd, Oxford

Contents

One thing the theatrical background gave me has been a great help. My family were trained for three generations to be 'servants of the public'. Trained for and dedicated to the part. When I am frenziedly tidying up, doing the flowers against time, giving the Aga a last-minute grooming . . . I am thankful to have belonged to a profession in which serving the public comes naturally. There are good days and bad days, just as in the theatre there are performances when the audience comes more than half way to meet you with warm and heartening enthusiasm and others when you seem to be performing to a house, or in our case a garden, full of suet puddings.

From Elizabeth's speech to the National Trust at the Royal Festival Hall, London, 25 April 1977. Quoted in Francesca Fraser-Darling, 'Subverting the Hortus Conclusus: the Brunners at Greys Court, Oxfordshire,' unpublished thesis, 2005

List of Illustrations

Family Tree

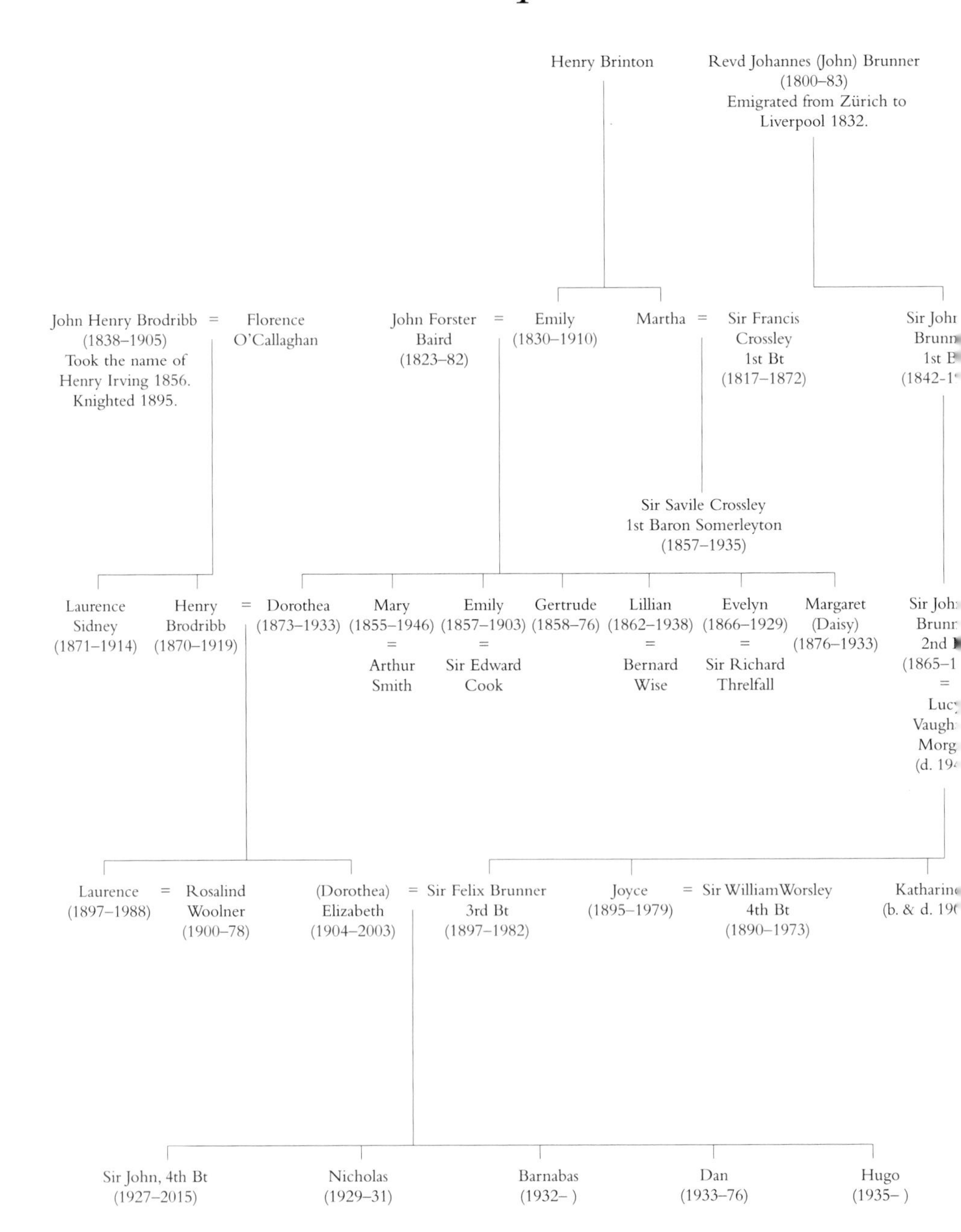

Henry Brinton
Revd Johannes (John) Brunner
(1800–83)
Emigrated from Zürich to
Liverpool 1832.
John Henry Brodribb = Florence O'Callaghan
(1838–1905)
Took the name of
Henry Irving 1856.
Knighted 1895.
John Forster Baird = Emily
(1823–82)
(1830–1910)
Martha = Sir Francis Crossley
1st Bt
(1817–1872)
Sir John Brunner
1st Bt
Sir Savile Crossley
1st Baron Somerleyton
(1857–1935)
Laurence Sidney
(1871–1914)
Henry Brodribb = Dorothea
(1870–1919)
(1873–1933)
Mary
(1855–1946)
=
Arthur Smith
Emily
(1857–1903)
=
Sir Edward Cook
Gertrude
(1858–76)
Lillian
(1862–1938)
=
Bernard Wise
Evelyn
(1866–1929)
=
Sir Richard Threlfall
Margaret
(Daisy)
(1876–1933)
Sir John Brunner
2nd Bt
=
Laurence = Rosalind Woolner
(1897–1988)
(1900–78)
(Dorothea) Elizabeth = Sir Felix Brunner
(1904–2003)
3rd Bt
(1897–1982)
Joyce = Sir William Worsley
(1895–1979)
4th Bt
(1890–1973)
Sir John, 4th Bt
(1927–2015)
Nicholas
(1929–31)
Barnabas
(1932–)
Dan
(1933–76)
Hugo
(1935–)

Introduction

A year or two before my mother died, in January 2003, I was looking for something in my father's desk – a pair of scissors I recall – in the library at Greys, when I lighted upon some pages in my mother's hand.

These pages turned out to be two distinct but overlapping accounts of her childhood, intended to be the beginning of an autobiography. The scope of the book, about which I had not previously heard, was sketched out at the beginning of each manuscript. It was to end with chapters on bereavement and old age, and with one entitled 'Reflections'.

In one of the manuscripts, the second to be written, my mother wrote: 'At this point Whitstable. See previous MS.' And indeed the second manuscript includes an account of her experience of the Mill House, Whitstable, which her mother had bought in 1907. MS2 continues with memories of her family and, in particular, of the books which were read to or by her as a child.

I read the manuscripts and was able to consult my mother about some proper names that I could not decipher. My reading led me to feel that, just as the Whitstable story was intended to be slipped into the narrative of MS2, so the other material in MS1 could sensibly be woven into it. I invited an experienced editor, Jan Greenough, to take on the task of producing a single typescript. This she very skilfully did. I then lightly annotated the text, to elucidate or add to the information in the story.

Finally I decided to give the book a title, introduce it, illustrate it, and add a brief account of my mother's life following her debut as a professional actress on the London stage, which she anticipates on the last page of her story.

Several people commented helpfully on my summary of my mother's life: my brothers John and Barnabas; my daughter, Isabel Sharp; Helen Carey, who like my mother chaired the National

Federation of Women's Institutes; Violet Miller, who arrived at Greys Court soon after our family did; and Joy Whitby. The Oxfordshire Federation of Women's Institutes has supplied valuable information.

My son Magnus copied many photographs from my mother's scrapbooks and family album. Anne Stamper, archivist of the National Federation of Women's Institutes, produced several photographs for me, as did Dee Bingham of Keep Britain Tidy. My brother Dan's widow, Helen Brunner, provided the photograph of the scene in the Antico Restaurant in Henley.

Producing even so short a book as this requires perseverance and I am most grateful to Helen Carey, Charles Pugh of the National Trust (he also allowed me to use Trust photographs) and above all my wife, Mary Rose, for encouraging me to complete the task and for preparing the typescript for publication.

Finally, I must thank my friend Simon Haviland, who has designed and produced this book, as well as making several suggestions for improving it.

Hugo Brunner, March 2010

Child of the Theatre

'We do not remember childhood – we imagine it. We search for it in vain, through layers of obscuring dust.'

Yet in a shaft of sunlight even dust gives a bright vision. Such highlights illuminate memory, and are as fleeting as English sunlight. What they reveal can be any sort of happening: sad or happy, strange or very ordinary, heartbreaking or hilarious. And of course there must be something of imagination in every recollection, for it is natural for human beings to garnish what they recall through their imagination; nature and nurture have combined to form what goes on in our minds, and inevitably influence the way we see and feel what goes on around us and what happens to us.

Born seven years apart, a brother and sister's impressions of childhood can differ extensively – a fact that Laurence[1] and I discovered in our eighties. So what I can tell my children and grandchildren will differ from what he (with such amazing total recall) told his – partly because my mind is far less encyclopaedic, less lucid and under more layers of obscuring dust. As the sunlight comes and goes it reveals, rather arbitrarily, events experienced in childhood and later life. Sometimes Laurence and I shared the same memories, but those seven years yield a very great variety of recollection of our immediate family background.

Family histories

If in the future succeeding generations want to know about Brunners and Irvings (or rather Brodribbs), Vaughan-Morgans and

1. Laurence Irving (1897–1988), theatre designer, artist and author.

Brintons and Forsters (or Bairds), there are many sources of information available. There is Stephen Koss's life of the first Sir John Brunner,[2] my brother's life of Henry Irving,[3] his subsequent autobiographical volumes published as *The Successors* and *The Precarious Crust,* and the so far unpublished ones in the archives of the Theatre Museum.[4]

When Felix and I married, we brought together two families which had each been established by men from nowhere. Johannes Brunner (Felix's great-grandfather) was an obscure Swiss citizen: he studied for the Zwinglian Church in Zürich, but on completing his training he had religious doubts. Feeling that he had disappointed his family in Bülach, he decided to go to England. In Liverpool he found the answer to his theological problems in the Unitarian community and the teachings of James Martineau. In time he became a much loved and respected schoolmaster of the academy he set up in Liverpool, St George's House. His second son, John Tomlinson Brunner, grew up to be a very successful businessman, an enlightened employer, a trusted and greatly valued member of the Liberal Party and a Privy Councillor, benefactor of countless good causes, and like his father an active and thoughtful Unitarian.

Meanwhile, a large family of yeoman farmers called Brodribb lived in the west of England. They must have been well established and respected in their modest fashion, but there were exceptions to the family record. There were some who emigrated to Australia – the circumstances of which do not ever seem to have been revealed – and there was one, Samuel (my great-grandfather), who proved extremely unsatisfactory. He married Miss Mary Penberthy from Cornwall, and in 1838, in a small one-up, one-down cottage in the main street of the Somerset village of Keinton Mandeville, she gave birth to a son called John Henry Brodribb, known as Henry.

2. Stephen E. Koss, *Sir John Brunner: Radical Plutocrat, 1842–1919,* Cambridge, 1970.

3. Laurence Irving, *Henry Irving: the Actor and His World,* London, 1951.

4. The Theatre Museum, in Covent Garden, London, closed in 2007. It was replaced by the Theatre and Performance galleries of the Victoria and Albert Museum in 2009. Its archives, now the V & A Theatre and Performance Collections Archives, are held in Blythe House in Kensington Olympia.

As Henry grew up, he had no doubts as to what he wanted to do, and a legacy from a Brodribb uncle enabled him to fulfil his ambition of becoming an actor. That was when he took on his stage name of Henry Irving.

Throughout the latter years of the nineteenth century both John Tomlinson Brunner and Henry Irving led lives that brought them into the mainstream of public life. Their biographies are records of dedication to the roles they chose to pursue. In 1895 they both knelt before Queen Victoria, the former to receive a baronetcy, the latter a knighthood, but I do not know if these two contrasting but equally to be admired grandfathers attended the same investiture.[5]

The Brunner family

For John Brunner the decision to accept the honour was difficult. His principles – surely influenced by his still close Swiss sympathies and heritage – made him reluctant to accept privilege. But, his first wife having died leaving a large family of young children, he was influenced to do so in gratitude to his second wife, who brought up the motherless brood and bore him three other children.

Sir John Brunner considered himself in some sense a public servant, despite considerable wealth and a prosperous way of life. In this he was faithful to the successful, non-conformist liberal tradition. The employer/employee relationship in the Brunner Mond works, in which he was personally very involved, remains to this day respected as a pioneer standard of good relations, built on trust, mutual regard and enlightenment. He built a school and/or a public library in each of the small Cheshire towns associated with the company, and his generosity is well recognised and documented at the Salt Museum in Northwich [now the Weaver Hall Museum and Workhouse].

Of course it can be said that he was only giving from the profits of his workers' labours. But I think the strong strain of his Swiss inheritance made him more motivated to create social equality through education, as his Liberalism did through politics. He was also

5. They didn't. Henry Irving was dubbed a knight on 18 July; John Brunner was enrolled as a baronet on 27 July.

a lively supporter of Home Rule for Ireland. One can reflect on the contrast between the four identities of the Swiss nation: German speaking, French, Italian and Romansh came together, not through bloody conquest, but spontaneously to create a peaceful *modus vivendi* in the centre of distracted Europe. Perhaps we in Great Britain should have given the same dignity and consideration to Scotland, Wales and Ireland.

The first baronet, Sir John Brunner, had a son called John Fowler Leece Brunner, the second baronet. He married Lucy Vaughan-Morgan, and they had three children, Felix John Morgan (3rd Bart), Joyce and Katharine. (There is available a short history of the Vaughan-Morgans, Felix's mother's family.)[6] The Vaughan-Morgans were well-established middle-class families who prospered in the world. Their many sons all came to London from Breconshire in the nineteenth century and flourished in the world of ironmongery and chemicals and trade papers. Some of them entered Parliament, and one became Lord Mayor of London – Felix, aged seven or eight, was his page. He was always supposed to be a bachelor, so after his death the family was greatly surprised to find that he was unexpectedly mourned by a widow. The whole family were, in both numbers and characteristics, very similar to Galsworthy's Forsytes.

The Irving family

My grandfather Henry Irving's circumstances were very different, as was his knighthood. He became an actor in the days when members of the profession were still regarded as 'rogues and vagabonds'. Despite Mrs Siddons and the Kembles and the Keans, it was Dickens's Crummleses from *Nicholas Nickleby* – warm-hearted, improvident, penurious, endearingly comic and economically extremely unviable – who represented most people's established view of the theatrical profession. Throughout his career Henry Irving strove to

6. A. Raymond Hawkins, *The Vaughan-Morgans of Glasbury: Their Tribulations and Triumphs*, Brecknock Museum, n.d. See also Austin Hudson, *The Brothers Morgan*, privately published, 1953.

1. Dorothea Baird, H. B. Irving and Laurence Irving, with a bust of Sir Henry Irving, 1896

create opportunities to bring actors and actresses into positions of respect and appreciation comparable to those of writers, artists and musicians. His acceptance of the knighthood was on behalf of the Crummleses and of, in his own time, the rapidly increasing number of gifted and distinguished figures making names for themselves in London and the provinces. The splendour of his Lyceum productions, as one succeeded another, gave new quality to theatrical tradition and marked a fresh conception of its potential. His own lifestyle was modest, and he died without leaving any wealth save that which had accrued to the status of his profession.

Henry Irving had two sons: my father Henry Brodribb Irving, and his brother Laurence Sidney. Both became actors in their turn, and like him, without demur, servants of their public. My Uncle Laurence's wife, Mabel, was also an actress.

My mother's background was different again. Her mother was Emily Brinton, whose family made carpets in Kidderminster. (Their most famous daughter was my cousin Mary Stocks, whose father, Dr Roland Brinton, had a general practice in Queen's Gate and cared for members of the Bloomsbury world; another of the family was a

2. Dorothea Baird as Portia

housemaster at Eton.) Emily married into the Forster family of Northumberland, of whom there seem no longer to be any relations. Coincidentally, just as my paternal grandfather had changed his surname, so my mother's father, John Forster, changed his name to Baird after inheriting a property called 'Thompson's Walls' up in the Cheviots. John Forster Baird was a gifted water-colourist and read for the Bar, but I do not think he practised much. He had modest private means, and so was able to pursue an artist's life, mostly travelling with his entire family in Switzerland.

After her marriage, my mother Dorothea remained an actress, but more for love of my father than for her own ambition or dedication to the profession. She did, however, have a very strongly developed sense of obligation to serve the under-privileged. While on tour with my father's company in Australia in 1911 she suffered a nervous breakdown, after which she gave up acting and devoted herself (and

3. H. B. Irving as Hamlet

to some extent her family) to concern for the socially vulnerable and unfortunate. She became the first woman Poor Law Guardian in St Pancras, and she pioneered the National Baby Health Council and the cause of unmarried mothers. She was a founder of the St Pancras School for Mothers in Ampthill Square, north of the Euston Road. She also went on rounds of the poorest district of Somerstown with the local doctor, who was a family friend, helping to deliver babies in appalling conditions.

When I married into the family of the Liberal Brunners I realised that the posters that were put up in our Bloomsbury windows at election times included the names and photographs of the Brunners' Liberal friends. One of these, Willoughby Dickinson, had a daughter the same age as Felix. From pramhood onwards, accompanied by their respective nannies, the two children went on outings together up Gloucester Road into Kensington Gardens.

Subsequently this lady reappeared as the wife of our son Johnnie's first housemaster at Eton,[7] remaining in post in the early years of the Second World War, well after what had been anticipated as retirement.

Dorothea Elizabeth

I always knew that I was a special child from one person's point of view. My father longed for a daughter, and when I was born he devised my names and what were to be my initials: Dorothea ('gift of God' in Greek) for my mother, of course, Elizabeth ('gift of God' in Hebrew) – making DEI my cypher. After my brother was born in 1897, my mother had expected another baby, a girl, the daughter that would have been the apple of my father's eye. But there was a miscarriage and it was not until 1904 that I was born, to be the object of my father's infatuation and delight. I often wonder what it would have been like, playing second fiddle to that elder sister I never had. She might have been more rewarding to him, but she couldn't have loved him more.

The night I was born my father was addressing a dinner of the Artists' Rifles, and returned to greet me at 2.00 a.m., the hour at which my poor mother was safely delivered. No question then of husbands joining in the birth: they waited in another room, listening anxiously until the nurse or doctor came to acquaint them of the outcome of the proceedings. The Artists' Rifles sent a silver spoon engraved with their crest and bearing the meaningful names Dorothea Elizabeth Irving. It eventually went missing during a visit at Greys after the war, like my little four-poster when we left our home at Gordon Place. I wish I had not lost it; but then I also lost the brooch presented to my mother by King Edward VII, after she and my father had given a performance of *The Lyons Mail* at Windsor Castle. The brooch was green and red enamel with ER in diamonds. Why, oh why, does one lose things that are precious or special or particularly valued?

7. Cyril Butterwick.

4. Elizabeth with her mother, 1904

I was born in April, when my brother, Laurence, was on holiday from Durnford, his prep school – a unique establishment kept by Tom Pellatt, a friend of my father's, at Langton Matravers near Swanage. Someone went to bring Laurence to see his small sister for the first time, and found him in the nursery stark naked, with all his clothes hung on the high fireguard before the gas fire. He felt he should air them before going to visit the baby, so that he would be specially warm when he re-dressed himself, and not make the baby cold.

I don't think Laurence had as good a start in life as I had: first babies suffer from all sorts of things that subsequent ones are spared. In my brother's case the birth process was a long one, and then my mother was unable to feed him herself for as long as she would have liked. Money was short, and the little household in a flat overlooking Tavistock Square needed the joint incomes of both parents to keep it going, so my mother had to go back to acting. My mother loved her son and must have bitterly resented the limited time she could give him and the bottles that fed him after only a few weeks of life.

By the time I came on the scene, finances were easier and my mother less pressed to work. She was still nursing me in December when she returned to the stage to play Mrs Darling in the first production of *Peter Pan* for the winter season: I was, I have been told, taken down to the theatre on matinée days for a feed. To this good start I attribute my fairly resilient physique.

I was fortunate, too, to be so wanted by my father: that knowledge gave me enormous satisfaction. There was a similar bond between my mother and Laurence, and the pattern repeated itself through the years to come: my father continued to be a glamorous and magical personality in my life. I loved my mother too, and when I was very small she would come to say goodnight to me in my cot, dazzlingly pretty in the evening gowns of the period. I continued eagerly anticipating these ravishing glimpses long after she had given up such youthful delights in dress. She was the least vain person imaginable, and as I grew up I gradually came to resent her lack of interest in her appearance and her refusal of social ventures in favour of good works and worthy causes. I concentrated on my father, and he took me with him on all possible outings, which were made into amazing treats by his very presence.

Earliest memories

My very earliest memories are associated with Bamburgh on the Northumberland coast – a place with links for all the Forster-Baird side of the family. I went with my parents when I was two years old and had my first two experiences that can properly be called memories. The first is recorded in letters by my father: one night I fell a very great height out of a shining brass bedstead. And I took my first staggering and frightening steps between a forest of seemingly very high chairs, occasional tables and hazardous stools, to be swept up into the oh-so-reassuring arms of my father, who for ever after was my great love and my hero.

My first home was 1 Upper Woburn Place, London. All the houses in Bloomsbury conformed to a pattern: up a few steps to the front door, the dining room on your immediate right or left, with your father's study behind it looking out on to a tiny garden or a mews if you were carriage folk. (But in Bloomsbury we were not carriage folk on the whole. The mews folk tended to live in affluent circumstances in Mayfair and Kensington and Bayswater.) Daddy's study had an oak overmantel, which moved house with us in 1911 to 7 Gordon Place, and eventually to our holiday home, the Windmill at Whitstable. The garden behind our house contained lilies of the valley; I specially remember a pair of fluted urns and a lot of gravel. On the first floor in front, with windows opening on to balconies, was the drawing room. Behind that was the children's room, shared for play by Laurence and myself. On the second floor was my mother's bedroom at the front; my father was very sensitive to noise so he had the quieter one at the back. On this floor there was the bathroom and perhaps a tiny bedroom for the cook. On the very top was my nursery-cum-bedroom at the front of the house. I remember a wall of cupboards with carved doors, then the two front windows, and a fireplace on the wall facing the cupboards: I was bathed in a tin bath in front of that fire. Behind the nursery was a tiny room for a nurse or governess, and a double room for the maids.

No. 1 Upper Woburn Place was a gloomy house. No. 7 Gordon Place was lighter and more cheerful and the move there was very exciting. Besides the almost exactly similar layout of rooms there was the added novelty of the 'telephone room'. This was on the ground floor to the left of the doorway from the hall down the stairs to the kitchen. The instrument was combined with a bracket on the wall. The receiver was shaped rather like the sort of container you used to throw dice in board games, and was hooked into a circular metal support with a flex attached. You stood – for me on tiptoes – pulled down the mouthpiece and lifted the receiver with one hand, your left, and with your right wound a handle on the other side of the bracket sharply, after which you waited for the voice before giving the exchange and number that you required. It was magical – just as the wireless was in the 1920s and the television in the 1930s.

5. With Norah Boyes, Princess Christian nurse, 1905

My earliest outings were undertaken in a pram made of light brown rexine with wicker-work arm rests and a brown rexine hood. My Princess Christian nurse, Miss Boyes – always called 'Bo-Yes' – was complementary to the pram in her brown caped overcoat in winter, and beige and brown uniform in summer. I was vaguely aware that the grown-ups who stopped to talk to 'Bo-Yes' were curious about me, for they probably recalled my mother's wedding at St Pancras Church eight years before I was born. My mother had been married from the house where her brother-in-law and sister, Mr and Mrs E. T. Cook lived; they had made a home for her when she became the toast of London's *jeunesse dorée* as the original Trilby.

My clothes were all made by 'little' dressmakers, and when finished were returned with a strong lingering smell of the oil stoves that heated their workrooms. The only exceptions were the 'jibbas' from Liberty's, which were my party wear. I specially remember a red velvet jibba with bunches of red cherries embroidered on the pointed yoke, and a black-and-white one for mourning, when Uncle Laurence was drowned – I wore it at the Theatrical Garden Party to which the Boucicaults took me with Violet Vanburgh's daughter Prue.

Occasionally a party dress was provided by being a bridesmaid, and a new pair of bronze dancing slippers would be forthcoming. My early years were made trying by the great wrestling that preceded any winter walk, when I was buttoned into gaiters that went up to the kneecap. The button hook was in constant use.

London walks

I can recall little of these early years. Shafts of light through the obscuring dust reveal my pram as it was pushed from 1 Upper Woburn Place down Southampton Row, via Russell Square (the east side, which was entirely occupied by a mammoth hotel), then right into New Oxford Street, with the de Bry Chocolate Shop on the north side, in the window of which huge rollers pressed out broad crinkly ribbons of chocolate caraque. I don't remember eating them often, but the occasional treat was indeed exquisitely delicious, light as air and fugitive and subtle. Then we would turn right again up Tottenham Court Road, passing Shearn's Fruit Shop that catered also for vegetarians, and the Cash Register Shop (very new and up to date, rather like computer shops are now), giving off a delectable smell of pear drops. Then came Heal's. Heal's sold children's four-poster beds and I had one of them when I was out of my pram and into long buttoned gaiters and walking the route. I still have the plush-backed chair from Heal's which was in my nursery.

Porter's Toy Shop on the other side of Tottenham Court Road was a paradise for children; later on, the assortment of cinemas that sprung up on the same side of the road afforded amazing spectacles which enchanted my brother. (My first recall of such novel entertainment was at the Scala Theatre, and was a film of the adventures of Edward Dunbar.)

Beyond Heal's was a turning to the right, which crossed Gower

Street and continued past a post office and a row of elegantly ornate Art Nouveau shops and flats, back into Gordon Square and Tavistock Square and so home. On this corner was Shoolbred's. From a very early age I was aware of a special interest in my visits: the daughter of Dorothea Baird and H.B. Irving gave incomprehensible delight to the ladies who worked on the ground floor immediately as we entered, supplying my mother with ribbons and veils and gloves. They each had a presence and a refinement that could have equipped them to be the best sort of governess or kindly maiden aunt. I wish I could remember all their names and assure them that eighty years later they are endearing reminders of my childhood. I do not recall a first or second floor in that shop, but if we were to order groceries we plunged into the basement where everything in our kitchen came from. Down there the congenial smells of tea, coffee, sugar, preserved and dried fruit, biscuits and jams and honeys and marmalades greeted one's nostrils. Even the ironmongery had its own special aroma – sharp and tangy with soap, turpentine and O'Cedar polish (very new), brushes and brooms and floor cloths.

Cullen's Stores had a branch next to Porter's Toy Shop, and their display of 'dry goods' was more arresting than what was to be seen in the Shoolbred basement. Their window was divided into small sections like patchwork, and each section held a different variety of appetising wares. Nothing was wrapped or packaged, but the square blocks could hold Bourbon biscuits, dates, various kinds of sugars and sultanas and currants, 'squashed fly' biscuits, a splendid jumble of oblong sections of chocolate, lentils, sugar candy, candied lemon and orange peel.

At Shoolbred's we left an order, and the delivery van would come the next day with the goods to be carried down the basement steps, so illustrating the formula 'families waited on daily'. The butcher and the fishmonger did the same, calling twice a day, once early in the morning to ascertain the household's needs, and again later, deftly delivering their awkward parcels, bloody or wet. The baker's calls were augmented by jolly characters proclaiming on their rounds that their muffins and crumpets were fresh and tasty – and indeed they were. They advertised themselves by ringing a handbell as they went

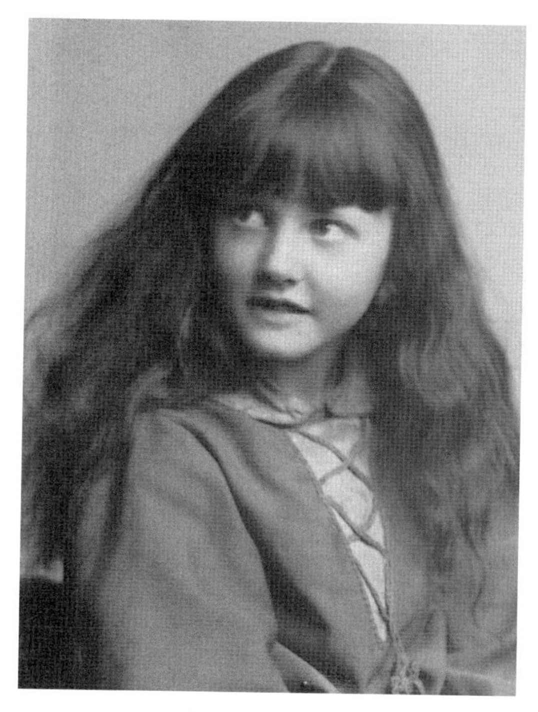

6. Growing up, *c.* 1909

along, the muffins and crumpets carried on their heads on a long tray, hygienically covered with linen cloths. Our dinner bell at Greys could well have been put to such use.

Cullen's Stores branches did not deliver, but it was more exciting and enjoyable to visit them, because of being able to watch the dextrous handling of half pounds and pounds of butter, slapped into shape with 'Scotch Hands', and the pounds of dry goods made up in cone-shaped thick blue paper containers. All this was done in the twinkling of an eye and accompanied by merry commentaries and much jokiness.

Childhood illnesses

I was not always well enough for such outings: illnesses were a large part of childhood. We all had to have measles, whooping cough, chickenpox and in my case scarlatina – a very dramatic affair with sheets steeped in a carbolic solution and hung over the door to the nursery. My father sent in a present every day, and only my governess, Miss Furrell, and my mother were allowed to run the gauntlet of possible infection. Dr Baker called every day – he lived in elegant Bedford Square, where there must have been mews, because he always drove to his patients in his own small horse-drawn carriage. I went bright red all over and caused great alarm. I don't remember how ill I felt then, but I do recall having measles. This was an extremely searching experience with the reward of a happy convalescence, during which for a whole week I was permitted only crusts of white bread spread with butter and washed down with milk. The latter was probably full of TB germs, to which my mother's prolonged suckling of me made me immune. I had both chickenpox and whooping cough while staying at Whitstable.

Various medications were administered frequently, sometimes in the hope of prevention. Being a skinny child because of the constant bouts of croup, I was considered delicate, and was ordered three pennyworth of cream every day with my porridge, which was delightful. I recoiled from Parish's Food and Scott's Cod Liver Oil Emulsion, but both had to be downed – the former through a glass tube, because it was said to damage the teeth. Castor oil was administered fairly frequently and Gregory Powders were, I suppose, a laxative. They were offered to the victim disguised in a spoonful of jam. Allen and Hanburys' Blackcurrant Lozenges were an invalid's treat, and oblong lozenges called *Magnum Bonum* and made by the same firm were highly regarded by both the doctor and his patient.

Croup was the real frightener and I was dreadfully subject to it. The remedy was something called ipecacuanha – drops of which were administered on lumps of sugar and had the effect of making one sick, so bringing up the terrible phlegm that constricted one's breathing like iron bars. Usually an attack was preceded by the common cold, for which pleasing treats such as hot honey and lemon drinks or blackcurrant tea came at bedtime. Friars' Balsam was inhaled from a jug of steaming water with a towel over one's head – usually at the onset of a cold in the head and in the hope of defeating an attack of croup. Earache could be nasty and there were two *vade mecums*: either hot oil or a very small boiled onion inserted into the affected ear, which, although comforting, were dangerous, often leading to mastoid operations that could prove fatal.

I do not remember being affected with such troubles at Whitstable or in the summer months. (Though after a bad bicycle accident at Whitstable, I had a suppurating left knee for weeks and screamed loudly at each day's dressing of the wound. Cuts and grazes were always painful, and caused prolonged pain, because the healing processes were very, very slow.) I expect the London fogs, thick, khaki-coloured and acrid, were bad for chests and throats. The smell of camphorated oil (rubbed on the chest and back) and the sweet herbal aroma of Friars' Balsam conjure up only Bloomsbury.

The adults were not immune to these ills. My mother and all her sisters (except the invalid one, my own dear Aunt Daisy) were terribly prone to headaches and bilious attacks, judging by their diaries and letters. Was it all caused by tight lacing, stodgy food, and lack of proper exercise and fresh air? Or was it really accounted for by menstruation (which was never alluded to directly under any circumstances)? 'Sick headaches' perhaps came from natural causes!

Household staff

Miss Furrell

When I was five my nurse, Bo-Yes, was succeeded by another Princess Christian nurse, Miss Parker. We were all terrified of her, including my father, and fortunately she was with us for only a year. Then a friend of Mummy and Daddy's told them about Githa Furrell, and she came to be my governess. I was fortunate indeed: from when I was six until I was eleven I was in the charge of her steadfast, loving, sensible and reassuring presence. She had a soft voice and a charming smile. She was adored by my father and she had enough sense of humour to enjoy his jokes when he burst in on us during lessons, covering her in confusion and totally demoralising her pupil.

I've no idea what her qualifications for teaching might have been.

Miss Furrell must have been my earliest companion in the exploration of the written word. *The Cock, the Mouse and Little Red Hen* was given to me by my father and was constantly re-read by Miss Furrell at bedtime or if I was ill. My father used to call me his 'little red hen' because the hen was always saying 'Then I'll do it myself' – he seemed to think I shared the same characteristic of independent self-sufficiency. The Beatrix Potter books were coming out throughout my childhood and each one was a tremendous treat, with the cuddly little animals in human clothes, the two plain pages between each written and illustrated one, showing the domestic life of Mrs Tiggy Winkle and Mr Jeremy Fisher's watery one, all so beguiling and representative of intense pleasure. Can Beatrix Potter ever have been fully aware of the inheritance she left for generations of children, given complete satisfaction and happiness by her books?

Miss Furrell's soothing monotonous voice was safe and comforting; each evening when I was in bed she would read from the Bible and hymns; she taught me my Catechism and made me learn the collects for each Sunday by heart. If I was restive then, now I am very grateful for her patience with what I fear was a reluctant pupil. Lesson books were *Reading Without Tears, Little Arthur's History of England* and *Mangold's Questions.* Copy books for writing began with 'pot hooks', and progressed to copperplate renderings of worthy sentiments and trite sayings. *The Children's Encyclopaedia*, like the works of Beatrix Potter, came out volume by volume during my childhood and helped to enlarge the boundaries of our simple schooling. It was the source of our rudimentary French lessons, with pictures in which we followed the fortunes of a French family like mine: mother, father, son and daughter. They shopped, travelled, enjoyed meals and holidays together, bought clothes, kept dogs and cats and made visits to the zoo. Miss Furrell's own weakness in mathematics joined in disastrous fashion with my congenital ineptitude at the subject, but at least we neither of us were troubled over our shared inadequacy. For art there were lovely Kate Greenaway painting books with uncoloured pictures of sweetly old-fashioned little girls and boys. Music consisted of the study of the piano works of Diabelli – 'Die a Belly' always made Daddy laugh.

7. With her much-loved governess, Githa Furrell, in Broadstairs, 1910

Miss Furrell slept in the room next to mine, and it was she who comforted me when I had bad dreams. From when I was about four, until I was nine or ten, I steadily dreamed the same dream or experienced the same revelation. This was of finding myself kneeling in the corner of a huge square picture or drawing. This was not a picture of a place or a person but a huge design based on a circle. Always crouching beside it or almost in it, was the tiny figure of myself kneeling in a curled up, awe-stricken position. It was a frightening dream at first, but gradually I got used to it and began to find it reassuring. By the time I was eleven it stopped. I used then to think about it and to accept that it had happened but had stopped happening. Fifty years later I read Jung's *Memories, Dreams and Reflections* and instantly recognised my dreams in his Mandela drawings. I felt again the strange contrast between the huge, complex, magical designs and the crouching figure of a child in a corner of the page. Needless to say, Jung's drawings did not include any child.

Walter

Another very important grown-up was Walter Collinson, a charming gnome of a man who had been my grandfather's dresser at the Lyceum and had looked after him in his rooms at Bolton Street and Grafton Street. When grandfather died Walter transferred himself to Daddy. He came at 10.00 a.m. each morning from Teddington to give my father his breakfast: two slices of toast, butter, marmalade and an apple – preferably a Cox's Orange Pippin. Walter can never have been home until midnight and must have left early to get to Bloomsbury by 10.00 a.m., and Sunday was the only day he did not come. He looked after all Daddy's clothes and even mended his socks. Each day he would put out his clothes and clean his immaculate, rather pointed button boots – if the weather was cold, spats would be at the ready too. My father would dress up to his shirt and trousers, and take his breakfast in his study on the ground floor in his dressing-gown. He would then write for two to three hours before going out for lunch, usually at friends' houses or at the Garrick or Beefsteak Club. My father would return home after lunch to have a rest before going down to the theatre; at 6.00 p.m. he would gulp down a raw egg or something similarly light to fortify himself until supper after the day's work was done. Walter would leave us at lunchtime, and reappear in the dressing-room at the theatre for the matinée or evening performance, with make-up, wig and toupé all laid out in readiness. Despite Walter's increasing years he ministered to my father, as he had to my grandfather, to the very end: he saw my grandfather die in Bradford in 1905, and my father at Cumberland Terrace, Regent's Park, in 1919.

Winnie

Winnie Gunn was our cook. Mother and Winnie between them ensured that we never had anything but delicious, good old-fashioned English food. Winnie had climbed the ladder from scullery maid to third, second and first kitchen maid in a great country house, where there was a formidable staff headed by an irascible cook. Someone called Lady Jean Bertie (pronounced 'Bartie') presided over this establishment. At some extremely inconvenient moment, the cook fell ill: Winnie (who was by that time first kitchen maid) had to cook a whole weekend's menu for a large house party. She herself was running a high temperature with an attack of flu: she literally tied herself to the legs of the kitchen table to keep herself upright, and nearly died of the pneumonia she developed as a result of these exertions.

My mother met her after her convalescence, searching for a new job in Mrs Hunt's Registry Office in Marylebone High Street. There was an in-built advantage to being a theatrical family in those days: the theatrical world had an appeal and glamour that made working for one seem romantic and exciting. Winnie could have returned to service in a much grander establishment, but chose to cash in her lot with us. We were fortunate, for she was a wonderful cook: her fish-cakes (small spheres, light as feathers and crisp outside) were perfect – I've never met any so good. She also made divine ice cream for great occasions; in winter her purée of chestnuts with orange salad and meringue was, and still is in memory, my favourite pudding. She composed it with infinite patience (dozens of chestnuts to be boiled and de-skinned and then put through a sieve, and the meringue whipped endlessly with the first mechanical hand beater – a great novelty at the time). I make it with tinned chestnuts in syrup put in a blender, and think with gratitude and affection of the labour it must have been all those years ago.

Winnie stayed with us until 1921 or 1922. She left only because my mother found her devotion to her was becoming obsessive and rapidly getting worse, so she had to cut this Gordian knot. I've no idea how it all came about, and as I grew older I often wondered about Winnie and asked my mother about her welfare. Whatever ended the relationship was irrevocable: no Christmas cards, no note when I got engaged, no further contact was ever re-established. If I blame my mother, I also blame myself: I was old enough at the time to have kept an independent link going. Winnie's brother-in-law was station master at Appledore in Kent. He had an only son, called

'Sonnie' by his aunt, who was the apple of the little family's eye. I tried to trace him in Appledore a few years ago but with no success.

Winnie was always ailing, yet I never remember her being ill. She was small and frail, pasty-faced with shining black eyes; her hair was combed back over an artificial rouleau and arranged in a bun on top. She was a firm believer in aspirin (then a fairly new drug) and she must have taken a bottle a week, as she always had a headache. This, alas, ruined her digestion, but somehow she battled on; my mother was most sympathetic and tried to ease things when she could.

Winnie had underlings, including a kitchen maid and a house parlour maid. I cannot recall the names of any of these except for the last two, a pair of sisters from the Leavesdon Orphanage School on the outskirts of London. They were called Martha and Maud in Dickensian orphanage fashion. Both poor girls must have put in time scrubbing the stone floors of the basement kitchen 'scully' and pantry, over which Winnie presided. Mummy also had a lady's maid, who doubled as her dresser in the theatre when she was acting.

All these props and stays on the domestic front must have been a great challenge and caused considerable anxiety to my parents. My governess received £36 a year for looking after me: wages and salaries were incredibly low by present-day standards.

Games and pastimes

By the time I came on the scene, my brother Laurence was already at prep school, but we played together in the holidays. In general he was always protective, and generously included me in many pursuits. First of these was his Pollock Theatre, in which he gave extremely ambitious productions of *The Corsican Brothers* and pantomimes. The climax was always a fiery one: he devised explosions which singed his eyebrows and hair, and were regarded with great alarm by Bo-Yes and my mother. My father enjoyed it all greatly: in their own childhood he and my Uncle Laurence must have created similar excited renderings with displays of pink fire and evil-smelling smoke to accompany the Demon King or various villains.

Later there were the 'Little Wars', invented by H. G. Wells.

Laurence's collection of lead soldiers – infantrymen, gunners, marines and cavalry – was extensive, and many battles were enacted on a landscape of old green velvet curtains, decorated with my wooden villages, farm yards, trees and fences. The troops were divided between us and duly arranged in embattled positions, with moves made according to appropriate lengths of string. The field artillery fired matchsticks, and as our resources were increased at Christmas and on birthdays, our heavier guns fired larger wooden bolts. Meekly I accepted those regiments whose moves were regulated by the shorter lengths of string, and I was rarely equipped with anything that fired more than a matchstick. Laurence's inventiveness and superior knowledge of the conduct of campaigns, as well as the greater mobility of his troops and very much better fire power, usually resulted in my poor fellows expiring in the folds of velvet, or being triumphantly surrounded and taken prisoner.

The final phase of our shared play came in the period when we kept white mice and rats. By this time we had moved to Gordon Place, and the first floor back room behind the drawing room had become our domain. Here, on a large central table, my brother had constructed a rat-and-mouse kingdom. Strong cardboard walls were erected around the table, and within was a fascinating complex of houses, palaces, pleasure domes, the lot. I am sure Laurence's subsequent ability to build stage sets grew out of this enchanted play area for our two rats. 'Ragtime' was a robust black-and-white rat, while 'Tango' was a creature straight out of Beatrix Potter – neat, well-groomed, petite and virgin white, with delicate pink nose and eyes. Small white mice were minor characters, who enjoyed running up and down cardboard staircases, over bridges, and in and out of wire cylinders and houses. Somehow they all got on together, and scampered over the sawdust paths and streets with obvious pleasure. The smell of this room eventually proved too much for the grown-ups; at the end of one of Laurence's holidays, which coincided with the death of 'Ragtime', the whole imaginative venture had to come to an end. But not before fate seemed to have declared its doom, as Tango, mourning for Ragtime, 'liked it not and died' too.

In those days Christmas was in no way regarded as it is now. Small girls contrived small gifts for the grown-ups such as penwipers, pincushions and 'hair tidies'. These latter were little bags or folded containers for grown-up ladies to hang on the mirrors of their dressing tables to take the daily combings of their hair. Our presents were given round a tree in the drawing room on Christmas Day: I never had a stocking until Brother decided I should have one. So that Christmas morning I awoke to feel, as other little girls I knew did, a huge lumpy object at the bottom of my bed. In the dim half-light I stretched down to explore and came on yes! a stocking. But attached to it outside was an enormous spider made of papier maché – the plastic of those days. All Laurence's tenderness and thought for his little sister were lost in a flood of fear and terror. It was far into Christmas Day before I had the courage to unpack my first and last stocking.

What seems so different about my childhood, when compared to that of our own children and even more so of our grandchildren, is the lack of playing with other children. Not that I yearned for the companionship of those of my own age – indeed I feared it. I went to dancing classes at the house of Sir Alfred Fripp, an eminent doctor with a vast mansion (or so it seemed) in Portland Place. Here Mrs Wordsworth conducted classes based on the needs of Sir Alfred's daughter Betty. Mrs Wordsworth was a terrifying figure, dressed in black like a witch, and very unsympathetic to those of her pupils not showing signs of becoming either prima ballerinas or dazzling hostesses in great houses. Being the daughter of the great H. B. Irving and Dorothea Baird failed to protect me from her sarcasm and sharpness of tongue. The very fact of being among a group of other children daunted me sufficiently to distract my attention and make me nervous and self-conscious. The few boys must have felt equally out of place. I had pretty enough dresses, but I suppose I had no variety with which to impress other little girls and their nannies. I was always thankful if an oncoming cold or threatened croup (or convalescence from one or the other) prevented my attendance.

The entire process was traumatic from the start. Because my party dress was necessarily thin, my clothing had to be reinforced with what were called 'spencers' – sort of jacket-vests – and shawls stuffed between me and my coat. My bronze dancing sandals, rather like unblocked ballet shoes, were delightful to dwell upon – but the clubs and skipping ropes were dreaded snares. The clubs were called Indian clubs and must have somehow been part of the legacy of the British Raj. With one in each hand we waved and twirled in unison to a musical accompaniment provided by a rather dim minion of the dreaded Mrs Wordsworth. My clubs were for ever getting out of time with the rest of my group, just as the skipping rope always became hopelessly entangled in my awkward, uncoordinated feet.

Children's parties were an extension of the dancing class, complicated by having partners left to choice and not regimented by Mrs Wordsworth. As I seldom knew anyone else at a party, I was rarely chosen willingly by any partner. And anyway if I was, the whole business of the Lancers and the Cotillion inevitably revealed my basic incompetence on the dance floor. The two memorable features of children's parties were the presence of the Pollock sisters, Elizabeth and Anne, and James Barrie (who acted as 'Nana' to the four Llewellyn Davies boys), whom we met in the bedroom where we all left our coats and changed our shoes. I can see him now, a small gnomish figure, kneeling at extended pairs of feet and adjusting buckled pumps with the most tender care.

I did tremendously enjoy the annual event of the Lord Mayor's Children's Ball at the Mansion House. This was a fancy-dress affair, which both Laurence and Felix must have attended before me. My mother was extremely clever at devising fancy dresses. Laurence is revealed in a photograph as a crusader or even possibly as St George himself. His chain mail was knitted with coarse string on huge knitting needles and painted silver; together with his wooden sword and the shield with a fine red cross it looked romantic and exciting. I think I went three times as a rainbow: I wore a dress of variegated silk wrung out in water and wound tight so that when dry it had a beautiful stripey sheeny effect – something like accordion pleating but less sophisticated. Then I went as Spring, achieved by trails of artificial spring flowers flowing over a simple green dress of soft Liberty material. But my final outfit, and the best of all, was Brunhilde. Again the string and knitting needles provided my splendid armour, a Wagnerian winged crown adorned my head and lengths of chiffon draped my armour. I remember (as Brunhilde) falling dreadfully in love with a medieval knight; I was subsequently allowed to go to a party and stay the night at his home, in Ealing, Turnham Green or Highgate. The hero, no longer in his glamorous fancy dress, was a total disillusionment, and the household bewilderingly uncongenial.

Perhaps I went for a fourth visit when my father was playing Charles Wogan in *The Princess Clementina,* because there is a photograph of me in a perfect replica of Wogan's black court suit, in which he stood in for the Pretender at his marriage to the Princess. The Lord Mayor's parties were fun because so many different sorts of people came together, and there were no groups of children all entwined among themselves, to the exclusion of others.

After these comparatively rare plunges into social life I returned gratefully to the domesticities of my own Bloomsbury world. I was then (as we all were) quite unconscious of that other Bloomsbury Circle, active in our very own square and in the process of becoming a literary and artistic legend.

Back at home Miss Furrell taught me to sew, to darn my stockings, to hem and run-and-fell and patch and make 'French' seams. She or Winnie taught me to knit. In the holidays Laurence played the piano, which was also a Pianola, and he had a gramophone well before the First World War started. It was because of his liking for music that our rats were called Ragtime and Tango, after the rhythms he found most popular: he had a special favourite called 'Hitchy Koo'. But I was never aware of any paucity of occupation, because there were always books.

Books

Bookshelves were always part of life. My father's study was the source of all reading matter, apart from my own nursery volumes: Marlborough prizes, books from studying history at Oxford, law books, criminology, theatre, Russian novelists, Russian history, lots about the French Revolution, and of course the ones he read to me.

8. 'Some academics . . . cannot quite explain how England, time and time again was rescued from a dreadful fate. I'd be content at any rate to give the credit where it's due, to Mr Baldwee, wouldn't you?' The man of many 'b's (baldrick, bowler hat, bald head, buttons, brolly, bag of bull's-eyes) created by H. B. Irving for his children in *Mr Baldwee's History of England for the Young*. Bertram Baldwee is depicted as an influential figure at the turning-points in his country's history. Laurence and Elizabeth 'looked forward eagerly to these sporadic cartoons with their assurance that behind our father's moody severity lay a love of folly for its own sake.' (*The Precarious Crust,* p. 163)

Strangely enough I never remember my mother recommending to me any reading matter except *Mrs Wiggs of the Cabbage Patch*. It was not until I was grown up that I learned of her affection for the contemporary domestic works of Charlotte M.Yonge – literary guidance for which I have been ever since deeply in her debt. It was my father who sent me an Everyman leather-bound copy of *The Little Duke* by C. M.Y., in which he wrote 'This was my favourite book when I was your age' – it came from South Africa in 1912, when I was eight. It instantly became my favourite reading, over which I shed many tears. The Little Duke Richard was the first person I fell in love with and I used to tell myself long stories about him as I fell asleep. The romance of the story and his striving for goodness impressed me so much that I truly believe I was always looking for that goodness and grace in all my heroes.

My father would always try to spare an hour to read to me between his afternoon rest and when he left for the evening performance at the theatre. *David Copperfield*, *Martin Chuzzlewit* and many others were read aloud in his study, which was surrounded by bookshelves topped with busts of Voltaire and others of my father's heroes. Most vivid is the remembrance of our launch into *Oliver Twist,* which reduced me to hysterical tears because the opening chapters were so terribly sad. My father wore hand-knitted waistcoats, as was probably then the fashion; I sat on his knee with my cheek pressed against the cable stitching. My tears fell silently at first, soaking into the knitting, and by the time my sobs broke out and my full reaction was realised by my distressed father, my cheek was indented with the pattern. From *Oliver Twist* we turned to *Nicholas Nickleby*, ever since my favourite Dickens. Characters like the Cheeryble brothers illuminated true goodness, standing out for me in those formative years. Someone said of dear Charlotte Yonge that she succeeded in 'making goodness exciting'. Dickens created other jolly, endearing, eccentric, tender characters that besides making goodness an excitement also made it enormous fun. I suppose I was about nine years old when we read Edgar Allan Poe. 'The Pit and the Pendulum' caused my father to compose a poem based on my difficulty in pronouncing certain words:

A little boy from Twyford (TWIFFORD)
Said we heard (HYERD) the bells aringing
And the Pendulum (PENDLEMUM) a-swinging
In the Tottenham (TOPMAN) Court Road.

How an eight-year-old survived my father's wonderfully dramatic reading of 'The Masque of the Red Death', 'The Murders in the Rue Morgue' and 'The Black Cat' I find it hard to imagine. Such tales produced no tears, but bedtime fears in plenty. The thrills were so great that I would never have acknowledged that our readings were the source of my fears, and risk having them stopped. Everything of course was read to perfection and the hour passed like lightning. When plays were in rehearsal and the theatre closed, our reading sessions could be longer.

Besides being an actor my father was a criminologist, and each morning he worked for a while, writing books on famous trials and various criminals, in which I took a lively interest. These, too, were read aloud: I vividly recall one story about a man who became impatient with his wife (who, if I remember rightly, made herself particularly trying to him) and in a fit of extreme impatience murdered her. Then he dextrously jointed her, tied up the remains in neat brown paper parcels and hired a horse-drawn cab. He then drove around London disposing of the packages over bridges, into dustbins, under shrubs, in public parks and in other obscure places. He was eventually traced and brought to justice. This kind of reading was very different fare from what Miss Furrell provided upstairs: Mrs Irving; Mrs Molesworth; the *Red, Green, Blue, Brown* and *Yellow Fairy Books*; Grimm and Hans Andersen; *Little Lord Fauntleroy;* and *The Secret Garden.*

I remember my mother reading to me only once, and that was *The Water Babies* and perhaps *Alice in Wonderland. Through the Looking Glass* I read for myself; indeed I read a great deal to myself, especially when Miss Furrell had gone down to supper, having tucked me up warm in bed and turned off the light. No sooner was she down the stairs than I was out on the landing, kneeling on the cold linoleum under the electric lamp, extending for half an hour my enthralment in *Stumps* or *Amelia and the Elves*. Looking back, I think my frequent colds and intermittent croup could be accounted for by the steadily increasing chill of those snatched sessions before Miss Furrell returned to the upper regions.

Family life

My brother was far more conscious than I am of having belonged to a theatrical family. By the time I was aware of the grown-up world, my parents had very much widened their circle. My father's interests were always wide: while reading history at Oxford he wrote a life of Judge Jeffreys, which was well received – but as a result he obtained a second-class degree when he should have achieved a first. He then studied for the Bar and joined the Oxford Union Dramatic Society at the same time. But when he wanted to marry he decided to change course: being my grandfather's son and himself a gifted actor, and having no private means, it was inevitably quicker to earn a living on the stage than to make his way at the Bar. But he never gave up his interest in legal and criminal matters; he continued to write books on criminology and edited Mrs Maybrick's trial for the *Famous Trials* series.

His socialising went on mainly at his clubs, where his friends were more inclined to be legal or literary than theatrical. At the portals of the Garrick there was always Monkey Brand. Monkey Brand was a popular kitchen cleaner and advertised by an anthropomorphous monkey figure. The guardian of all the Garrick's members must have been the original of this widely known character – certainly he was its double. What went on, what treasures the club contained, how or when the members ate, or sat at ease far into the night talking, no women – let alone children – had any idea. The shades of Dickens, Thackeray, Trollope and my grandfather made it a shrine of London's folk memory – but it was only to Monkey Brand's little glass cubby-hole, halfway up the steps on the right-hand side, that anyone but members and their male guests ever penetrated. My mother joined a circle of interesting women who lunched once a month in the Grill Room or a private room at the Ritz.

My mother always had her breakfast early, in bed, and Miss Furrell and I had dining-room breakfast, after which we did lessons in the dining room at Upper Woburn Place. I suppose it had been swept and dusted very early indeed. Lunch was served in the same room, always for Miss Furrell and me and sometimes for Mummy and Daddy too.

Our domestic life was made extremely demanding by my father's acute sensitivity to street noises. He slept each morning until 10 o'clock and rested each afternoon between 3.30 and 6.00 p.m. During the prohibited hours everyone in the house had to be on the alert for the various sounds common to London streets in those days. Vendors of lavender or muffins, repairers of cane chairs or knife sharpeners, indeed most of the activities that made up the well-known prints of 'London Cries' – all these made an amount of noise that was intolerable to him. They were joined by one-man German bands, barrel organs (the predecessor to the gramophone which when wound played large perforated disks in a manner similar to the rolls on the Pianola), harpists, violinists, Salvation Army bands, our neighbours blowing shrill metal whistles to call taxis, and worst of all barking dogs – all these had to be kept at bay, when appropriate, urged to go to another street, and if necessary bribed to leave my poor father undisturbed. When we read *David Copperfield*, the cry 'Janet – donkeys!' always reminded me of the combined efforts of our whole household to shoo away street criers and bands while my father had his afternoon rest.

Miss Furrell and I had tea, and my father took his raw egg at 6.00 p.m., before the theatre. There was milk and biscuits for me at 7.00; and Miss Furrell and my mother sometimes had supper at 7.30.

People came to tea occasionally, and sometimes (when my father was only rehearsing) there were dinner parties. During these Winnie would tear herself away from the frenzied activity in the kitchen to smuggle ice cream (made with time-consuming effort in a bucket) or meringues whipped by hand, or that heavenly chestnut purée, upstairs to me in my four-poster bed. Miss Furrell pretended to look askance at this indulgence but she and Winnie lived in a state of armed truce combined with mutual respect.

My mother was a gifted but not a dedicated actress. She fell in love with my father when he was at New College and she was living with her widowed mother and invalid sister at 9 Rawlinson Road in North Oxford. They acted together in OUDS productions, which she followed up by joining Ben Greet's Touring Company. By chance when *Trilby* was being cast by Herbert Tree's production, photographs of my mother in Ben Greet's Company appeared in some illustrated magazine. These pictures demonstrated her extraordinary resemblance to the illustrations of du Maurier's book. She was chosen to play Trilby and made an instant success.

All the time, however, what really counted in her life was the romance of falling in love with my father. She was totally indifferent to the praise her performance merited and received, and after she was married she seems to have had no personal ambitions. She acted with my father on and off until she had her nervous breakdown and moved into a new world of aiding the underprivileged. She was not I think a feminist, nor was she in any direct way concerned with any political party, but through her fresh interests she met many distinguished and able women who were active on the fringes of the suffragist movement.

Her special interest in these matters could, I think, be traced to one particular event. Before Martha and Maud came to join Winnie in our household, a previous servant (also an orphan) was taken away ill in the middle of the night. She was indirectly the object of my mother's labours on behalf of the Unmarried Mothers, and of yet another cause: on my mother's desk I saw leaflets headed 'Bastardy Bill'. For years I considered that this must be a famous music hall star. I knew all about music halls because sometimes my father would do a tour of the Provinces between his own productions in London, performing a short one-act play which my grandfather had done called *Waterloo*.

When I was still sleeping in a cot with high sides I remember the rapture of seeing my mother, looking beautiful in an exquisite, scintillating evening dress of brocade covered in roses, coming to say goodnight as I stood up grasping the protecting rails. My father would tell me of how, when he came back after the theatre with friends, he would bring them upstairs to see me asleep. As I got older

I tried to stay awake so as to be conscious of these visits, and tried arranging myself romantically to gratify them. Of course, odious child that I was, I hardly ever brought off this dreadful conceit. I am sure I was more often found curled up in a ball with my mouth open, to be viewed by an unimpressed but sympathetic audience.

On these evenings when friends came back after the theatre my mother would compose little suppers with a chafing-dish – lobster newburg perhaps, with champagne. The household never waited up for them. In those days it was unusual for middle-class matrons to do anything in the kitchen, but somehow my mother had learned to be a skilful cook, and often prepared supper for my father after the theatre. When she gave up acting, my father sometimes used to go to the Garrick Club to unwind after the play. His half-bottle of champagne was not a great extravagance in those days: he found it wonderfully therapeutic after the stresses and strains of a day's rehearsals and an evening performance, especially after a first night. Following one such first night he and my mother were asked out to some grand supper party to which they went reluctantly – first nights were particularly demanding. After the first course my mother's neighbour turned to her and found her in tears. He pressed her to tell him what was the trouble, and she told him, 'Harry must always have champagne after a first night and *no one* is giving it to him!'

Whitstable

From 1907 we holidayed at Whitstable: two semi-detached cottages joined into one house, and a windmill. The house had a kitchen, scullery, dining room and drawing room, with a little hall and a staircase leading to five bedrooms. There were two little communicating bedrooms at the back, and Mummy's room and Daddy's room were both on the front. The maids' bedroom was over the scullery with a window looking towards the windmill. There was a privy sheltered by a pergola in the yard where the coal was stored.

The furniture included some massive wooden armchairs and rockers brought back from a Canadian/American tour: they were agony to fall against, having the sharpest corners ever, but great leather cushions gave comfort to the occupants. They were monolithic and I often wonder who bought them when the cottages were pulled down and the house that Arthur Knapp-Fisher built round the windmill replaced them. The bedroom suites were made of white-painted or brown-stained wood. There were always two maids, so Laurence and I and Miss Parker (soon replaced by Miss Furrell) must have fitted into the two tiny communicating bedrooms. The bathroom had a painted bath, a basin and a loo, with bottles of Sanitas and Pond's Extract so placed that one could study all the fascinating details of the uses they could be put to.

At Whitstable there were bookcases on either side of the fireplace in the drawing room and dining room. Mostly the books were 7d copies – neat blue or red volumes. *Life on a Pound a Week* was an enthralling study of families who had to live on this modest sum, who submitted their budgets and told the tale of their brave housekeeping. Mrs Ewing and her mother's *Parables from Nature*, *Red Pottage* by Mary Cholmondely, the *Elizabeth and her German Garden* books – at Whitstable it seemed that reading was of the current popular feminine kind, so I think the choice must have been my mother's ,with the exception of Conan Doyle.

We spent most of the long hot summer of 1910 there. The social life of a small seaside town involved many fêtes, sales of work, pageants and so on. Floats were arranged, giving a fine variety of interest to carnival processions. For me, the long hot days meant for some time a change of routine, with two hours' rest in the tropical afternoon heat, and being allowed to sit up later in the evening.

The change from London to Whitstable was measured in the early morning, lying in bed listening to the scrunch, scrunch of wheels and horses' hooves mounting the gravel of Borstal Hill, instead of the sharp clip-clop and rattle of London traffic on Bloomsbury streets.

Whitstable characters

Whitstable was bought by my parents for £400 – the two cottages, the windmill and five acres on top of Borstal Hill on the road leading out of Whitstable to Canterbury. I think I was four when we first went there, but there was a short time (perhaps while we were moving in) when I stayed in rooms with Bo-Yes in a house belonging to the family of Plymouth Brethren at the foot of the hill. I imagined the Brethren to be some sort of nautical fraternity, and missed the imagined conviviality and jollity I connected with Drake on the Hoe.

Frank Tyers had made a corner in real estate at this particular end of Whitstable. He had acted in grandfather's Lyceum Company and then in my father's company, and used to ride on horseback down to Whitstable from the Lyceum on Saturday nights. He was established in a small manor farmhouse at the bottom of the hill. He was something of a speculative builder for there was another member of the company – Miss Poppy Davis – living in one of his houses with her ancient mother and two or three sisters. Mr and Mrs Carson and their daughter Dot occupied another of Mr Tyers' houses, and Miss May Davis, a cousin of the Davis family, lived in a bungalow on an island site where the Canterbury Road was joined by the road to Seawater. Somerset Maugham had recently spent his boyhood holidays from the King's School, Canterbury, in the rectory on the road into Whitstable.

9. Whitstable Mill

There were other characters whom we came to know: Dirty Walter and Old Hammond brought a Dickensian touch to the neighbourhood, the former living in a hut on Duncan Down and the latter occupying a minute cottage halfway up Borstal Hill, so dirty it had to be pulled down when he died. Just below the rectory there was a house full of belligerent and frightening women with no noses. Our gardener, Mr Richards, came up several days in the week: he was a frail little red-faced, blue-eyed man who was in delicate health. He had a formidable, high-bosomed wife. Her hair was put up in a huge bun composed of thick plaits. She sailed along in profusely buttoned boots with a train of Miss Richardses behind her, the youngest of whom 'Heva Hannie Maud' was about my age and was always referred to by her three names. Richards' delicacy of constitution was manifested by seizures of what came to be called 'sideways loops' (the aeroplane was beginning to introduce new phrases into the language) from which he was revived by my mother with nips of brandy. The 'loops' could occur with great regularity and my mother was teased for her soft heart and supposed gullibility. But she had a pretty shrewd knowledge of the poverty line on which the Richards family existed, and she delighted in her ministrations.

We kept chickens at Whitstable, which Mummy, wearing her sunbonnet, cared for enthusiastically on summer visits. But as she was inevitably committed to spending most of her life in London, Mr and Mrs Wheeler, who lived opposite in a cottage at right angles to the road, came to help with them the rest of the time. The eggs were sent to her in London in strong wooden boxes, with each little nest for a brown egg lined with protective felt or thick flannel.

My most vivid and sustained memories of Whitstable are linked with Miss Furrell.

Travel

Our journeys to Whitstable were conducted by a four-wheeler and by the S. E. Dover and Chatham Railway Company from Holborn Viaduct. Black shiny-domed trunks, stoutly strapped-up wicker baskets and square hat boxes made up the luggage. There always seemed to be some able-bodied man or boy on the London streets who would help load and unload it all. There was a very special smell about the four-wheeler, for leather, corn, the horse itself and the stable made a rich amalgam.

Another sort of smell assailed the traveller on entering a train, mostly of the upholstery material, coal fumes from the engine, pipe, cigar, cigarette smoke – and a distant whiff from the convenience at the end of the corridor. The journey seemed unendurably long, though books and comics and bull's-eyes or Harrogate toffee helped to pass the time. Chatham was half-way, and at Faversham the end was near, with the marsh and its tiny Seasalter Church bringing us past the beach where we bathed in summer to the Whitstable station perched up above the main street. Here another 'fly' would be taken. Always in the station itself and its approaches there was a most dreadful 'lavatory' smell, which was never remedied until the station was demolished and replaced further down the line.

My other taste of travel came in 1911, when I went to meet my parents on their return from the Australian tour. This was a brave undertaking, as they left the house in charge of Mrs Fortescue, Miss Poppy Davis's sister. It was an eventful time: she and Miss Furrell fell out, and it was suspected that Mrs Fortescue consoled herself for her beleaguered life with alcohol, the proof of which was a residue of bottles in her wardrobe. Winnie too resented the poor lady, who was always late for meals – at breakfast the excuse was that a stay lace had broken and delayed her.

How successful the Australian expedition proved to be I don't know, but it was my mother's 'Waterloo' as far as the theatre was concerned: it was there that she had her nervous breakdown. But on their return Miss Furrell and I were taken down to Toulon to meet the Orient line ship, the *Orsova*, on its return journey.[8] My cousins Harold and Gertrude Hartley accompanied us and great fun the whole expedition proved to be. The night on the train, the waking up in Toulon, where the streets were lined with roses, the drive up to a fort and the reunion on board ship with my parents was memorable. Then we had all the fun of a voyage round by Gibraltar, which

8. Her parents' tour also included New Zealand; they were away for a year from May 1911.

10. Reunited in Marseilles with her parents on the *Orsova,* May 1912

was a wonderful time of spoiling and indulgence: soup was brought round to all the passengers at eleven in the morning. I loved Gibraltar, which proved to be a source of enamelled silver bangles and intricately inlaid boxes. Even Miss Furrell relaxed and lost her heart to Roland Pertwee, who was the company's juvenile lead.

Church and faith

Miss Furrell was my constant companion, and she made sure that on Saturday mornings I learned the collect for the coming Sunday. Then on Sundays we would go to church together at Christ Church, Woburn Square. The Revd A. M. Bestic was the vicar and obviously was pleasing to Miss Furrell. We were if anything nearer to St Pancras Church, where my parents had been married, and both my brother and I were christened there (by the then vicar, Luke Paget, who moved on to be Bishop of Stepney) but Miss Furrell must have given preference to the slightly cosier ambience of Christ Church. One of the churchwardens was Mr Dibden from Russell Square, who read the lessons admirably.

I had a Sunday coat and hat, always based on a wire circlet that cut my forehead, and in winter I wore the inevitable gaiters, and woolly gloves that made one's freshly cut nails (a regular Saturday night event) feel horrible. The services seemed endless, and the Creed, especially the long version, was quite incomprehensible. But the hymns were lovely and *Jerusalem the Golden* was quite my favourite. Mr Bestic's sermons were not too lengthy, and as long as I sat still I could observe my fellow members of the congregation and try to imagine what their families and homes were like. The ladies' hats and feather boas and the romantic charm of some of the younger men provided endless preoccupation (I was very open to, but critical of, male charm; I suppose because my father set such high standards). Miss Furrell had thoroughly grounded me in the catechism and I knew my way round the Prayer Book and *Hymns Ancient and Modern* so I felt at home.

The congregation was large by today's standards, and from a child's point of view it was all dreadfully dull and only came to life with the jolly hymn singing. One had to sit still and one had to try to listen, both of which are good things to learn to do. They were I suppose early lessons in patience and perseverance, but to a child submerged in a forest of grown-up persons, long church services were a severe training. The benefit of course was that one had the magically beautiful words of the morning and evening services of an unrevised Prayer Book built up perforce in one's memory bank. Our weekly visits to church became part of the accepted pattern of life, both in London and Whitstable. Nobody at home seemed in the least interested in them and they were a sort of secret shared between Githa Furrell and me, irrelevant to anything outside our nursery life.

I had the usual complement of godparents: My godfather Henry Kemble, an actor and a friend of my father, became a Roman Catholic at about the time I was born. My godmother Irene Vanburgh was of a good Church of England family: her father was a Prebendary of Exeter Cathedral. She was kind and affectionate, but I didn't see much of her. My other godmother died when I was eighteen, leaving me £100, which was a tremendous inheritance and was spent on a squirrel fur coat.

But Miss Furrell was my real spiritual influence: she was a devout churchwoman and went mysteriously to 'Early Service' before we had breakfast on Sundays. To her I owe loyal allegiance to the Church of England and an affection which always seems to be mixed up with her kindness and goodness. She loved her church so trustingly and transmitted to her unrewarding pupil a sense of the tranquillity of faith. Githa Furrell lived to be a great age. She made me aware from childhood of how a simple faith can illuminate quiet lives in humble places.

My father was an agnostic, but not an atheist; he loved Shakespeare and the English language. The whole vast panorama of history, and the lessons it taught of human frailty and ambition, heroism and treachery, comedy and tragedy, was part of his stock in trade as an actor. I think he stood in awe of the destiny and meaning of life; as a loving father he made God seem likely to be loving and understanding and a refuge, at least to me.

My mother on the other hand was rather like the father in Rose Macaulay's book *Told by an Idiot*, which is about a man who started life as a Church of England clergyman, and in the course of raising a family changed his allegiance from one branch of the Christian faith to another, to the bewilderment of his confused and hard-pressed family. Whatever he happened to be at the time of his children's birth, the baby was given a matching name – so a daughter born while he was a Unitarian was called 'Una', and so on.

I first became aware of this when she took me to sit at the feet of the Revd Mr Cranshaw at the church in North Audley Street (Miss Furrell must have been on holiday). I was astonished at the contrast between Bloomsbury and Mayfair. A crowd of us had to stand in the extensive lobby, while the verger stood by the doorway into the church proclaiming 'Pew-holders only', 'Pew-holders only'. Then, as the bells neared the end of their ringing, he would relent and it became a free-for-all, as the non-pew-holders trouped in to fill up the gaps in the congregation. I was later amazed to see that when the obviously greatly revered Mr Cranshaw started preaching, my mother drew out a notebook and pencil and took down extensive notes of his sermon. I remember feeling very embarrassed because she seemed to be the only person in view occupied in this way.

At about the same time – after rather than before – there was a Bishop of London she regarded with favour, but then she moved on to Maud Royden, an eminent preacher in one of the nonconformist congregations. She was devoted to Luke and Elma Paget and remained friends with them for many years, and in some way she was acquainted with Bishop Burge of Oxford. She took me to stay with the Burges in the palace at Cuddesdon after my father died, and I always remember the beauty and peace of the buildings – now all sadly burnt down – and of the garden. So she must have been anchored in the Church of England, but after my father died she went off at a tangent into Women's Free Masonry and even became slightly involved in Rosicrucianism and numerology. The casting of the horoscopes occupied her considerably and when our son Johnnie was born, she carried him about calling him 'my darling little Gemini'.

The wider family

Grandmothers

There were two grandmothers in our background: one was my mother's mother, who lived in North Oxford. I think she was in the early stages of senility, and flitted in and out of the rooms in her house, a mysterious, shadowy figure in black with a lace cap. However, the house, 9 Rawlinson Road, was the most dear and welcoming place to visit, because of the welcome from my youngest aunt, Daisy, who ran the home from her wheelchair.

The other grandmother was Lady Irving who occupied a flat in Connaught Road, Folkestone. Grandmother Irving (who was born Florence O'Callaghan) was terrifying. She must have once had the red hair that is apt to occur in the family, but by 1908, when I became aware of her, she was surmounted by a rich auburn wig. I think she must have shaved, for a perfunctory kiss from her positively prickled a tender young skin. She had a penchant for purple, which extended in various shades from her face powder to her underclothes and outer garments, and she affected toques and feather boas rather in the same manner as Queen Alexandra and her daughter-in-law, Queen Mary. Subsequent history shows her to have been a good mother to her two sons (my father and my Uncle Laurence). She brought them up alone, since my discouraged grandfather, Henry Irving, abandoned her at Hyde Park Corner one night in 1871. She was no good as his wife: a sort of proud, fierce Dickensian character, who despised the theatre and considered she had married beneath her.

If she ever loved anyone, I suppose she loved her sons, of whom she inevitably became possessive, with the unfortunate result that she was hostile to her daughters-in-law. As a child I remember her coming to Gordon Place, and later to Cumberland Terrace in Regent's Park for my brother's wedding; these visits oppressed my mother and brought on her dreaded migraines. I would sometimes receive letters from her, always written in purple ink, in a firm, characteristic handwriting that never changed. She attended my wedding in 1926, and outlived her sons; she must have been quite a feature of the retired circle of neighbours in Connaught Road until she died aged 88. As the traffic conducts me round Hyde Park Corner, I always feel that grandfather's spirit must take comfort: it was in a taxi passing the Royal Artillery war memorial that Felix proposed to me – a moment in time that set up nearly sixty years of loving companionship and understanding. Would that grandfather and grandmother had found such fulfilment.

The red hair, a tendency to mothering sons and the final role of robust nonagenerian were my inheritance from Florence O'Callaghan – all of them kinds of good fortune. But how I wish she had loved and understood my splendid grandfather and given her sons something they must have missed grievously in their fatherless childhood.

Uncle Laurence

One uncle (on my father's side of the family) and six aunts (on my mother's) were supplied. My father's brother, Laurence, first came into my life in 1911, when my parents were in Australia with their

11. At South Hampstead High School, where she became a pupil in May 1914

company, and he came to take a look at me from time to time. Like my father he was enormous fun, and threw himself into making a child laugh outrageously and quickly escape grown-up controls. I remember going to Gilston Road, where he and Aunt Mabel lived, alas without children of their own. I was somehow aware that this was a sorrow, and that Aunt Mabel withdrew herself from children's pursuits; looking back I can well understand this. Uncle Laurence would have been an adorable father – there seemed no dark shadows in his life such as came and went in my father's, whose devastating moods permeated the house when they fell upon him, and which were intensified by illness for the last few years of his life. It was to Gilston Road that Uncle Laurence would take me for afternoons in 1911, running and leaping down the quiet South Kensington roads, making all sorts of fascinating jokes and on one occasion ending up with a bonfire in his garden. Alas, the wind carried the smoke directly into Aunt Mabel's bedroom where she was resting, and as a result the subsequent tea party was somewhat subdued.

He must have encouraged me to write – perhaps a diary of my doings for my parents in the antipodes, or some imagined story. Anyway, that afternoon he gave me a box file like a book, on the spine of which in spidery writing I inscribed 'Doub's* collected works'. In this box I kept the letters I received from father and mother on their Australian tour, and from him when he was touring South Africa in 1912.

Uncle Laurence died when I was ten – drowned when the *Empress of Ireland* sank in the St Lawrence River, when he and my Aunt Mabel were returning from a theatrical tour of Canada. That was when I learned about mourning, because I had to have a black liberty jibba with a white collar. At his memorial service I remember some Japanese people came in full national dress, to honour him for his translation and production of a play called *Typhoon*. It all seemed so improbable and extraordinary and sudden that for a child the sorrow was lost in the event.

Aunt Mary

The six aunts in themselves covered a generation. My mother's eldest sister Mary was eighteen years old when she was born, and my youngest Aunt Daisy was born three years after her. Aunt Daisy was the only one who was our special aunt: I suppose she and my mother shared their childhood together, and so were closer than any of the seven.

Aunt Mary is recorded by her own family, and in her turn wrote a life of her distinguished husband A. L. Smith, one time Master of Balliol College, Oxford. She became dedicated to the cause of infant welfare in the slums of Oxford, just as my mother was in St Pancras.

* 'Doub' was the name I went by in childhood, which survived among my own family and a few old, old friends and their children until today. Elizabeth was the name I was to go by, but its pronunciation somewhat defeated me when I began to talk and refer to myself. 'Loub-la' was my version and for some reason that became 'Doub-la', which shortened to 'Doub' became the final usage.

This created some jealousy on Aunt Mary's part. She was a somewhat vindictive lady, and at one point there was nearly a law-suit in the family: this was because Laurence and the youngest of her children, Hubert, were at a crammer together when they were 17; they fell out and Laurence blacked Hubert's eye. Aunt Mary subsequently spread gossip in Oxford about the reasons for Laurence leaving Wellington at a comparatively early age. My father was outraged, and though he was disappointed in his son's poor academic progress at Wellington, he stood by him under his Aunt's calumnies. For some years there was a severe rift between the Smiths and Irvings, but before that I remember awesome visits to King's Mound and being terrified by Aunt Mary. Later on, in the early 1920s, I used to stay with Aunt Mary's daughter Gertrude and her husband, Harold Hartley, at 7 St Cross Road. Gertrude was the eldest of the seven Miss Smiths and I had been her bridesmaid in 1906 at the age of two.

Aunt Mary was especially in awe of her cousin Savile Crossley – subsequently Lord Somerleyton. My grandmother Emily Jane Baird had a sister who was Savile Crossley's mother, so Aunt Mary and Lord Somerleyton were first cousins. No family event, be it wedding or funeral or celebration, was considered complete by Aunt Mary without the presence of Cousin Savile. As far as we were concerned we saw little of him, though I think he was at my wedding. (The Crossleys, like the Brintons, made carpets – in Halifax.)

Of the Northumbrian connection I knew nothing except our association with Bamburgh. A local heroine, Dorothy Forster, was in some way a forebear, and my mother was christened after her – Dorothea Forster Baird. The Smiths have a house in the village to this day called St Aidans, and in my extreme youth I remember that was the name given to 9 Rawlinson Road. Lord Armstrong, who restored Bamburgh castle, was a friend of my father and mother. He was fondly regarded and called 'Wa-Wa', and had a kindly, homely wife. Together they created Cragside in Northumberland (this great house now belongs to the National Trust) and were most tender in welcoming my brother there for a prolonged stay when he was recovering from TB during the First World War. I cannot remember how the two families came to meet.

The Smith family included nine children: my first cousins, Lionel, Gertrude, Molly, Dorothy, Maggie, Biddy, Rosalind, Barbara and the battered Hubert. At the age of four I acted as bridesmaid again, this time to Molly, when she married Fred Barrington-Ward. I was always told that my mother, who was in charge of me on the occasion, was shamed by my screaming and having to be removed. Through my tears I avowed that I should have behaved differently had my father been there.

Cousin Dorothy was a very endearing person, and I saw quite a lot of her and Robin Hodgkin at Bradmore Road in Oxford in the 1920s, and also during the Second World War at The Queen's College. Her son Teddy has strengthened the links in a subsequent generation. But one way and another all the nine Smith children touched my own life over the years. Johnnie, together with David Cairns, Barbara's son, paid a call on Aunt Mary (then a very great age) in the 1940s, when they were both undergraduates; they shared the experience of hauling her out of her fireplace in the nick of time when she had a fall.

Aunt Emmie

My mother dearly loved her sister Emmie, who married Uncle Teddy – Sir Edward Cook – who in his turn was a father figure to my mother, since her own father died when she was in her early teens. My mother lived with the Cooks in Bloomsbury when she went to London to play Trilby. Because of their London life and the circles in which they all moved, she and Aunt Emmie developed common interests. Like Uncle Laurence and Aunt Mabel, the Cooks had no children, which was a deep disappointment to Aunt Emmie. My mother told me that she was thankful not to have to tell Aunt Emmie that I was on the way – child bearing and its denial to her being such a painful subject. She died shortly before I was born, of the cancer which had also claimed John Forster Baird.

Emmie was one of the first women journalists, and I have some of her articles bound at Greys. There is one describing my mother as a schoolgirl being taken abroad by the Cooks: faced with the magical sights of Italy and the Alps, she yearned only for the joys of the senior forms at the South Hampstead High School. Uncle

12. Sir Edward Cook (1859–1919), Liberal journalist and author, married to Aunt Emmie Baird

Teddy was a distinguished journalist, whose biography and own life of Florence Nightingale are also at Greys. He was editor of Liberal London newspapers in the 1890s and in the early years of the twentieth century. His sister, Mrs Alec Vincent, was also a gifted writer and a loved figure of my mother's. Her younger daughter Peggy was Robin Duff of Old Meldrum's mother, and I was her bridesmaid in apricot satin trimmed with brown fur and a new pair of bronze sandals.

Aunt Evelyn

Aunt Evelyn married a Birmingham engineer called Threlfall. I think she had four children, two sons and two daughters, but I do not remember ever having much contact with them.

Aunt Lilian

Aunt Lilian married Bernard Wise, who had been a brilliant undergraduate at Oxford. He became Attorney-General of New South Wales, and they had one son called Tony. Uncle Bernard always seemed to have something of an unfortunate aura, and his early promise petered out. But on a visit to England when I was eight or nine, he took me to the Zoo and gave me a copy of the *Just So Stories,* which Miss Furrell read to me – a pleasurable experience to both of us. Tony grew up to be a slight object of ridicule in the family – very conventional and pompous.

Aunt Gertrude

Gertrude died of diptheria or scarlet fever while still in her teens, when the family were living at Teddington. The only real record of her life is found in Aunt Emmie's fascinating journals,[9] which Aunt Lilian sent me to read in the 1930s, when she was heading towards a slow decline into senility. I think they passed into the keeping of Diana Coutts-Trotter, the daughter of Gertrude and Harold Hartley. They make absorbing reading and should be put into circulation in the family: they describe the whole family's travels round Switzerland in the 1880s. John Forster Baird, though a barrister, nevertheless made time for several such journeys over the years, during which he painted delightful water-colours of alpine scenes. The little girls had the benefit of his instruction in sketching, and were all good water-colourists. Gertrude's paintings, however, were in a style quite different from her sisters' more conventional efforts: had she lived she could well have been a distinguished artist. Aunt Emmie's diaries describe the illness and death of this gifted aunt, who was a sad loss to her sisters and parents. She is buried in Teddington churchyard.

Aunt Daisy

Finally there was Aunt Daisy, the youngest and dearest. When she was seven years old, she contracted infantile paralysis, now known as poliomyelitis: it was obviously a very severe attack. There seems to be no record of the details of the illness, but it left her severely handicapped at a time when remedial treatment did not exist. She was

9. These were among the sources for a full account of the Baird family given by Elizabeth Nussbaum in *Dear Miss Baird: a Portrait of a Nineteenth-Century Family,* Charlbury, Oxfordshire, 2003.

13. Aunt Daisy with (?) her cousin Francis Crossley, 2nd Baron Somerleyton, and 'Duck' at 9 Rawlinson Road

totally paralysed from the waist down, so that her legs never grew properly, and she could use only three fingers of one hand and two of the other. Every morning she had to be hung on a sort of tripod before being buckled into a tight steel corset. She spent her days in a carrying chair, or in a bath chair when she was taken outside for fresh air. Each afternoon after lunch she would be laid on a sofa in the library or drawing room for a rest.

As she grew up she managed to overcome her handicaps, developing a delicate, pretty, very individual handwriting (she became a great letter writer to a wide circle of friends) and learned to play the piano and sing. Had she not suffered that tragic illness, she would surely have been the most gifted of the sisters. Yet her personality was one of the most endearing and inspiring imaginable: her understanding of and sympathy for the young was an unquenchable spring. She read widely, and enjoyed regular visits to the Oxford theatre until she became steadily frailer in her fifties. Strong commissionaires carried her tenderly from her bath chair to her seat in the dress circle, and she would enjoy every moment of the performance, most especially if it were at the time of a Gilbert and Sullivan D'Oyly Carte season. She was a discerning critic of acting and production, but I can't remember if she had the same enthusiasm for concerts.

After my grandmother died, she felt that her home in Rawlinson Road was too big for her, so she decided to take in paying guests (this was always possible in Oxford). She enjoyed the friendships such a way of life afforded: immediately after the First World War she took tremendous pleasure in housing undergraduates. The university was faced for some years into the 1920s by a shortage of accommodation for the heavy influx of students in 1919, and the post-war expansion of numbers could not be matched by the necessary building development. It was during that war and in the 1920s that I spent most time at Rawlinson Road. Aunt Daisy's sympathy with the young and her wisdom and example and zest for life – together with her delicious sense of fun – made her house a haven of peace, common sense and liveliness. By today's standards there was a large staff: a cook and house parlour maid, and another young person who was at the beck and call of the other two – my grandmother's companion Miss Price, who stayed on after grandmother died in 1913.

That Aunt Daisy was a child of grace was manifest, but I do not remember her as being committed to the comforts of religion. Perhaps there was a privacy about her faith that was painful: in her adolescent years there must have been unimaginable frustrations, for she would have been a ravishing girl, and she had an innocently flirtatious streak, which made her immensely attractive to intelligent men throughout her life, despite her disabilities. The churchgoer in the household was Miss Price, who was an ardent Anglo-Catholic member of the congregation of St Philip and St James. The family had an amused regard for this busy little lady and her parish activities, and there must have been a fondness for her to be kept on as part of the household after grandmother died.

The crowning jewel of the household was known as 'Duck'. Duck was Miss Anne Baynton, a Worcestershire farmer's daughter, who was taken on as nurse to look after Aunt Daisy following her illness. For approximately fifty years Aunt Daisy and Duck faced life together, each drawing from the other's strengths that deepened and enriched their individual characters. I do not think they ever slept apart in all those years unless Duck was occasionally ill. But providence was good to them, and Duck was remarkably robust; she outlived Aunt Daisy, even though she was some twenty-five years older. She did suffer from mild diabetes towards the end of her life, but even this did not develop until a year or so before her 'loved child' (as she always called my aunt) died in 1933.

Duck was the one who had a natural simple faith rooted in the rustic parish of her childhood. Her prayer book and Bible were in daily use, and the calm and tranquillity that seemed to envelop her were matched by her beautiful caressing Worcestershire voice. She was mainly without education, for her schooling must have ended at the age of twelve, or at the most fourteen, but she assimilated interests from my aunt year by year, and became discerning and discriminating in all sorts of subjects. Her gentle manners, tact and sensitivity never failed; to be with her and Aunt Daisy was a unique experience, to be remembered as an example of perfect goodness. Nothing 'goody goody' or priggish – but a glimpse of the lives of the saints.

Friends of the family

Although I had no children to play with (apart from my brother) I never felt lonely, though it is mainly grown-ups whom I remember. There was of course a host of members of my father's company. Uncle Teddy lived almost next door. Then there was Mrs Aria[10] and Miss Wootton, Sophy Hall and her husband Sir John. There was

10. Eliza Davis Aria, author of *My Sentimental Self*, was a friend of Sir Henry Irving. She remained close to the family after his death.

A. E. W. Mason, who wrote books, and Mr Courtenay who, like Uncle Teddy, was a distinguished journalist. I remember the Howard de Waldens in a huge house across the south-east corner of Belgrave Square. My father used to go there a lot, and sometimes took me with him, awestruck at the splendour.

There were people who gave children's parties – Lady Colefax and the St John Hornbys and old Mrs Gough in a house by Westminster Abbey. There were my godmother Irene Vanburgh and her husband 'Dot' Boucicault, and Violet Vanburgh her sister, who was married to Arthur Bourchier, another actor manager. She had a daughter called Prue, who was older than me and of whom I stood in awe. The Roland Brintons in Queen's Gate also had a younger daughter called Jo, who was exactly my age: her elder sister Mary and her husband John Stocks were young grown-ups, but they were just as intimidating to me (though they were very kind to Laurence when he was at Oxford taking early exams in 1915).

There were also the Trees, who seemed to live in the dome of His Majesty's Theatre. When my parents were in Australia Miss Furrell and I were summoned there to spend the afternoon with Lady Tree and her grown-up daughters. I was allowed to paint (in more Kate Greenaway painting books) while Lady Tree read aloud 'The Marsh King's Daughter' and the Hans Andersen story of the girl with seven brothers who were turned into swans: in order to turn them back into their human form she had to make coats for them in a limited number of days. She managed to make six coats, but the time passed before she could put the last sleeve in the seventh coat, and so that one brother always had a swan's wing instead of one of his arms. I found this story very moving.

When my mother gave up acting, she made many friends who took an interest in the same issues which then occupied her. There were great contrasts among her range of friends and colleagues. Bertrand Russell's first wife Alys (Pearsall-Smith) was one of the founders of the St Pancras School for Mothers, as was Adèle, wife of Sir Carl Meyer. The Rendells who lived in Russell Square – Edith and her sister who founded the Caldecott Community – linked up with the Roland Brintons. My mother was courageous when courage was called for in the various campaigns she embarked on, and she and my father were both regarded with great affection by the McKennas and the McIvers. The McKennas had four handsome sons, of whom the First World War took a terrible toll.

The McIvers were quite extraordinary and very endearing, and I would sometimes go to their house with my parents. Lady McIver was a Montefiore, and my mother and Robin Montefiore (a nephew of Lady McIver's) were both concerned in good works. The McIvers had two daughters called Marjorie and Natalie, both rather frail, delicate, gentle and willowy. In turn the two girls (who were in their twenties when I first remember them) had two governesses. It was a household where praise was unstinted – you came away from it feeling 'you walked on air'. It seemed as though all the assembled ladies went out of their way to express their wonder at their guest's goodness, beauty and intelligence. The food was incomparable and laughter and high spirits abounded. Lady McIver spoke with a strong rolling of her Rs and for some reason, unfathomable to me, was spoken of with fond amusement as 'Grrroans and Grrrumbles'.

I once went and stayed with them in a house at Sunningdale which they had taken for the summer. For once I was without Miss Furrell, and was left in the care of Marjorie's and Natalie's two governesses. It was an enchanted world. I loved slipping into bed between the exquisite, heavily embroidered linen sheets; the constant flow of praise; the promise of treats (blackcurrant ice cream brought to me in bed from the dinner party going on below); the life of the school room, in which the mature Natalie and Marjorie still seemed idyllically happy, with the loving, cultivated and lively governesses. When I first remember the McIvers they lived in Mayfair; after Felix and I were married they moved to 32 Great Cumberland Place, by which time Marjorie had married Harry Phillips and had a son. After we left London (just before the Second World War) I lost touch with them; I think the Phillipses lived at Englefield Green.

The whole family taught me how important it can be to praise children – and indeed grown-ups too. It wasn't flattery or gushingness – it came through warmth of heart, and a vision that could see only the best in those they regarded as their friends or trusted employees.

Lady McIver's own family lived in a splendid house in Portman Square, South Side, and Robin did much social work in the East End.

Another family generous with praise and affection were the Henry Heads. He was a distinguished neurologist at the London Hospital and Ruth, his wife, had been the greatly respected headmistress of a Girls' School. Her name before her marriage was Mayhew and in Francis Kilvert's *Diaries* he records visiting her parents' North Oxford house and going to say goodnight to little Ruth! Her brother Arnold was a friend as well.

Far away across London Felix had been raised in South Kensington, a nest of Vaughan-Morgans, and in Cheshire at the heart of nineteenth-century industrial England. In London the Brunners were neighbours of a legal family called Romer. Sir Robert Romer married Betty, daughter of Mark Lemon, the founding editor of *Punch*. Their daughter Nellie married Frederick Maugham (Lord Chancellor in the thirties) who was at Trinity Hall, Cambridge, with Felix's father. In 1924 Felix and I met at their house.

Schooldays

In 1914, when I was ten, it was decided that I should go, like my mother, to the South Hampstead High School for Girls. Miss Barton, Mummy's own headmistress, was still there to welcome me and Miss Furrell would make the journey with me on a No. 8 bus from St Pancras Church every morning. She would collect me at 4 o'clock for the return journey.

Miss Furrell's grounding proved sufficient to keep me in touch with the curriculum, and I basked in the general excitement created by my being Elizabeth Irving, the daughter of Dorothea (Dolly) Baird, who had been an outstandingly enthusiastic and successful pupil within the memory of many of the present staff.

I was blissfully happy in a low form conducted by the very kind and gentle Miss Towsey. We performed a play at the end of my first year, and I took a leading role (on the strength of my theatrical lineage) as Pearl, a sea-nymph, in *A World Beneath the Sea*. Again my mother's resourcefulness in fancy dress played a large part in my enjoyment of

14. With her father and brother, Laurence, 1915

the occasion, completed by my father's attendance at the first performance. My head was certainly turned by the admiration and acclaim that I attracted.

After the summer holidays I was moved up a form into the charge of Miss Cooper. Here life was very different, for Miss Cooper was a great contrast to Miss Towsey. Now there was no petting, no misty-eyed memories of my mother's prowess, no acknowledgement of the glamour of the name of Irving. Younger than the rest of the form and anyway far less able, I sank to the back row, languishing and disconsolate, defeated by mental arithmetic, the mastery of the French language (Miss Cooper's special subject) and by the initial approach to the comprehension of what was embracingly called 'science'.

All that remained was the use of the pen. Miss Furrell's copperplate copy books were by now considered 'old hat', and writing at the High School was based on Elizabethan script. I took to this like a duck to water, and was able to raise my stock a fraction with Miss Cooper by being awarded the form's prize for writing. Indeed, it was the only prize I ever won at any school: by now we were just entering the First World War, and it had been patriotically decided that no actual prizes would be awarded, only certificates, for the duration.

The Garvin girls were scattered throughout the school and pursuing academic success beyond its walls. Kitty was my contemporary, with Una and Viola in the giddy heights of the Upper School. Their father was the greatly respected editor of the *Observer*. Enid Marx was a glamorous contemporary, brilliant at gym and athletics, and at art and school work generally. She was endowed with a neat, boyish figure and was allowed to wear her gym tunic most dashingly short, displaying elegant legs. She was all I wanted to be. Unfortunately, as I was growing fast, my own gym tunics were always bought to allow for further growth, so that they hung very dowdily well below my knees. My own legs were as good, if not better than anyone's (considered to be a fortunate inheritance from my father's long, well shaped ones) and I was determined that my display should be at least as generous as Enid's. This I achieved by tying the girdle of my gym tunic very tight and looping up my tunic into a sort of pouch pleat all round my circumference. This succeeded in displaying my enviable extremities but made my figure appear somewhat strange. Any similarity to Enid's neat, trim style failed to be achieved and my mother and Miss Furrell both strongly disapproved of my idiosyncrasy. I don't think I ever explained to them that I would like my gym tunic shortened.

For the first year of the Great War, life continued as usual, with the daily journeys to the High School, and our spring and summer holidays at Whitstable. Laurence was extracting himself from a crammer in order to get into Oxford, and the grown-ups were manifestly worried, shocked and bewildered by what was happening. Then bombs began to be dropped on London by Zeppelins, and the prospects for theatrical people looked extremely uncertain.

I remember spending a large part of one night sitting on the flour barrel behind the kitchen door, while Zeppelins droned among the searchlights and the sound of bombs falling rumbled round about. At the St Pancras School for Mothers, Mummy had made a friend of Lady Meyer's sister, Mrs Ethel Thompson. She lived with a daughter and a son in North Oxford, and her daughter Sylvia was just about to move on to attend the Oxford High School, having been for a year at what was then called Lynam's and is now known as the Dragon School.

My mother had taught at Lynam's before she went on the stage, and she knew Ethel Thompson as an enlightened, lively, highly educated person, whose marriage had come to an end leaving her responsible for the upbringing of her children. Mrs Thompson already had a god-daughter living with her, and was planning to expand her intake: this was to include me and another friend's daughter. Sylvia was a forceful, extremely gifted and beautiful girl, a year and a half older than me and much more sophisticated. She had been expelled from Lynam's for blacking the eye of the headmaster's favourite girl pupil. Lynam's had always had a certain number of girls among its pupils and 'Skipper' (as the headmaster was called) had his favourites among them. Sylvia was not one of these; though Mrs Thompson and Mr Lynam remained on good terms, and Geoffrey Thompson, who was my age, continued at the school, Sylvia was withdrawn. She was sent to be a thorn in the flesh of the then headmistress of the High School, Miss Haig-Brown.

In February 1916 I arrived at the school. Joy Grimming and Enid Hirsch were already installed at Northmoor Road and each morning we bicycled off to the High School, then at the bottom of the Banbury Road. Sylvia's high spirits and unconventionality, combined with intellectual ability beyond her years, caused great problems. Sent out of class for insubordinate behaviour, she amused herself by dressing up the busts of the Roman Emperors that lined the school's long main corridor, in all the hats, mufflers and coats from the pupils' cloakroom. Then when all the school was practising for the end of term concert, and the combined young voices were reaching full pitch in 'Where the bee sucks, there suck I', the bold adventuress let off a stink bomb. This proved too much for Miss Haig-Brown, who had no sense of humour, but probably did have an eager waiting list of what might well be easier pupils. So at the end of the summer term we were all *persona non grata,* with nowhere to go.[11]

Mrs Thompson was resourceful and resilient; she had a flaming row with Sylvia and then went into session with her friends and contemporaries from Somerville days, Miss Taylor, an eminent historian, and Miss Hugon, a French scholar. Somerville College was about to be turned into a hospital, and its dons would be without work. So it was agreed that they would combine with Ethel Thompson in teaching her problematic quartet, adding to their number Mrs Haverfield, wife of the Professor of that name, to teach mathematics and Mrs Hunter, who was a classics teacher. Ethel Thompson would supervise prep and be responsible for discipline and for some of the teaching.

If only we could have been aware of the opportunities we were being offered and could have been mature enough to take advantage of them – we would have been the most fortunate children in England. We attended gym classes given by a splendid Oxford character, Miss Gamlen. Rosina Fillipi (married to H. M. Dowson, cousin of the poet Ernest) lived in Charlbury Road: she had played Madame Vinard (the original) in *Trilby* with my mother, and was a fine actress and teacher of acting, based on her excellent book, *Hints to Speakers and Players*; at the Randolph Hotel a member of the dreaded Mrs Wordsworth's staff came once a week to give dancing lessons. We were enrolled in all these classes, and Enid's mother, Mrs Hirsch (who had also found lodgings in Oxford), gave us piano lessons from time to time. Another friend of Mrs Thompson, Mrs Stanford, and her daughter, lived in lodgings in Ship Street, which they shared with a distinguished authoress, Netta Syrett. Elaine

11. During the Easter holidays, on 22 April 1916, Elizabeth made her stage debut at the Savoy Theatre, London, walking on with the guests in the wedding scene of *The Bells*. Her father played Mathias, the role which had made his father famous. She later told the *Observer* (12 December 1920): 'I think I had to say three words: "Good morning, Burgomaster."'

Stanford shared some of our classes but actually went to Wychwood School.

We rode on Port Meadow and skated there in the very cold winters; we swam at the Rhea swimming pool and did art at Lynam's under Mr Sturt. We also painfully went to Lynam's to act as the boys' dancing partners when they were being instructed, reluctantly, in ballroom dancing. In summer we rowed and punted and went for constant picnics, lugging two huge baskets with double wicker lids down to Tims's Boat House near the Dragon School. When we parted after two and a half years of this idyllic life, Sylvia Thompson and Joy Gunning were sent to Cheltenham Ladies' College, and Enid Hirsch and I to Wycombe Abbey. Sylvia subsequently wrote a novel[12] about her childhood which was published by Blackwells: in it she calls herself Elizabeth and me Dorothea.

I could not respond intellectually to Mrs Haverfield, Mrs Hunter or Miss Hugon. But I think that Miss Taylor, however discouraged she must have felt over the powers of her youngest pupil, could glimpse that she had sown a seed on the smallest possible area of promising soil. For a twelve-to-thirteen-year-old to be taught mediaeval Italian history by an Oxford don was not a common happening; I have always been grateful for having been at the receiving end of such an unusual experience.

Mrs Thompson's own contribution in teaching us English Literature was one of the most fortunate things that ever happened to me. What she imparted complemented all that my father had started me off with: Jane Austen, the Brontës, Mrs Gaskell, Thackeray, and Erskine Childers' *The Riddle of the Sands*. Stevenson and Kipling were always being read aloud, and one was allotted time in the day to read to oneself.

Mrs Thompson read aloud quite differently from my father. She was lively, intelligent, totally unhistrionic. For Jane Austen and Mrs Gaskell her twinkling blue eyes would sparkle with delight as she read quickly in a well-modulated voice. She, like my father, must have been good at cutting as she went along: I don't think either of

12. *The Rough Crossing*, Oxford, 1921.

them could possibly have read every word in each stout volume to have got through as much as they did. I was always encouraged to read as many books as I could, and Mrs Thompson was well disposed to surreptitious reading in bed after one should have put out one's light. I suppose I was an advanced reader for my age. I remember *Anna Karenina* by the light of a torch under the bedclothes in Northmoor Road when I was just fourteen. Sylvia, two years older, was much more sophisticated: she liked Meredith, Henry James, Compton Mackenzie, H. G. Wells and poetry. She had completed her classical eighteenth- and nineteenth-century novelists with her mother at an earlier age, and looked rather condescendingly on our enormous pleasure on hearing them. *Anna Karenina* was my first step towards a more mature kind of reading – and my introduction to the rich store of Russian novelists and other writers that has been so absorbing ever since.

Life was turbulent in Northmoor Road, for Sylvia and her mother exasperated each other. I was used to the uncertainties of my father's temper but both his and Mrs Thompson's gifts and insights and splendid sense of humour lessened the traumas of their own rages and impatience. With no private means, and his own family and his company depending on the success of each production, my father lived in a permanent state of stress and anxiety. Mrs Thompson also had much to try her: her sisters had all married prosperously and her brother administered some part of Kenya with considerable success. Her own finances, however, were uncertain, and she had to bring up the children without much help or support. She was fortunate in enjoying extremely good health and had two devoted maids, Rene the cook and Amy the house parlour maid. Both were great characters, Rene being an opera singer manqué, and Amy the kindest of persons and always cheerful.

In mid-September 1918 I was to begin my first term at Wycombe Abbey. By then the family were established in a rather charming turn-of-the-century house on Harrow Hill, 10 Sudbury Hill – the move there from Gordon Place had been accomplished during my absence in Oxford in 1917. There was no Miss Furrell to guard my treasures during the move, for when I went to Mrs Thompson in

1916, Miss Furrell went to Greenwich to make munitions for the duration of the war. So much of my childhood disappeared – the little four-poster (I had probably grown out of it) went, and so did a treasured collection of Russian decorated wooden plates and dishes. These had been sent by a friend of my father's who was in the Embassy in St Petersburg, and who for some reason wrote to me constantly throughout the revolutionary years of 1917 and early 1918. I can still see his letters in my mind's eye, written on squared paper and describing events which are now famous. I think he was a friend of Marie Lohr, a charming actress and my father's leading lady in a play called *Le Grand Seigneur,* in which a very young Basil Hallam played the part of a romantic young man at the time of the French Revolution. By 1917 Basil had been killed in a barrage balloon. But Daddy's friend in Russia has remained a mystery – perhaps he was a military attaché.

Dark days

My father's 'paroxysms' and moods of dark temper were often laughed about, but illness made them worse, and in the last four years of his life they made us all unhappy and frightened. At about the same time as I went to Northmoor Road, Daddy had closed his theatre and gone to work in naval intelligence. He was only forty-five and his services were appreciated in a department headed by his friend, Admiral Sir Reginald Hall.[13] But he was already suffering from Hodgkin's Disease, and my poor mother must have had much to trouble her as the war went on and Laurence was with the Royal Naval Air Service.

We spent the summer holiday of 1918 at Bamburgh in one of the parts of the castle let to visitors – the Library House I think. August was cold and wet in that northern area, my brother was recovering from an operation for TB glands in the neck, and my father became mysteriously unwell and impatient. Laurence was, however, sufficiently convalescent to lead me on a great climbing excursion right

13. Admiral Sir Reginald Hall (1870–1943), director of Naval Intelligence 1914–18.

round the huge rock on which the castle stands. I was extremely frightened as the rock fell away beneath me and we scrambled from ledge to ledge round the great girth that upheld the castle. This feat accomplished, we anticipated congratulations, but received only condemnation and rebuke. It was a hazardous enterprise for which my parents and the local inhabitants would hear no excuses.

In mid September Winnie accompanied me south to London. I said goodbye to her there and made my way to Wycombe Abbey. My arrival was extremely unhappy: no one had any idea of the sorrows and anxieties of the summer or of the parentless send-off from Marylebone Station. But there was no lack of caring in Butler House, with its pretty William Morris orange-leafed wallpapers and curtains, and my housemistress, Miss Lang, was kind and gentle. The house contained several very nice senior girls whose parents knew mine: Angela Elton (whose father had been Laurence's housemaster at Wellington) and Joan Hopkins (whose mother knew mine through St Pancras local government) were prefects – and indeed Angela was head of the house. But my friendships were limited to the two or three girls who started school in the same term as myself, and they had no appeal. After my idyllic life at Oxford the shock of boarding school was harsh, and night after night I cried under the bed clothes, trying not to hear the snoring of the other occupants of the dormitory.

After I had set off for Wycombe, my parents returned to Harrow. Things gradually got better, and my father was well enough to visit me at Wycombe later in that first autumn term and again the following spring. However, after those two terms I was kept at home for the summer term and the summer holiday to be with my father. We spent it at Whitstable, and when he was feeling well enough my father taught me the history of the French Revolution. During that summer he got steadily thinner and thinner; when the gales blew in from the north, the rattling of windows in the night drove him mad, and his irritability was almost continuous. Meanwhile Gladys Cooper's house in Cumberland Terrace, Regent's Park, had become available to us, and my mother was busy arranging yet another move, from Harrow to that house.

By this time I think she was desperate. She surely knew that

Daddy had not long to live and it was all a race against time. She was aware of the bond between my father and me, and I suppose keeping me at home to be with him was all she could do to make him happy. I was fifteen, ignorant of the reality of the situation, frightened and desperately inadequate. I had no regrets about missing a term at Wycombe, but I was bewildered and distressed by my father's rapidly declining health. When September 1919 came, the family were installed in Cumberland Terrace, and I went back to school.

There at Wycombe in October I was called out of class and told I was to go home: my father was very ill. I was put on the train and told that arrangements had been made for me to stay with Mrs Aria, whom I had last seen in her flat in Fitzroy Square. I succeeded in taking a taxi to that address, only to find that she no longer lived there. I telephoned home for directions and learned that she had moved to Albion Street, north of Hyde Park. Eventually I reached her safely, and she told me how ill Daddy was.

I went to see him the next day. The drawing room, which held all his bookshelves, was an L-shaped room on the first floor; his bed was in the smaller part of the L. He looked terrible but was able to smile and hold my hand. He died that night.

The whole dreadful sorrow was eased for us all by the presence of Nurse Riches who had been with my father for several weeks, and stayed on to care for my mother and reassure and comfort us all. I stayed with Mrs Aria for several days and she took me to buy mourning clothes at Debenhams. It was all quite dreadful – the strange house, the arrival of my father's mother (never an easy event for my mother), the terrible unhappiness. I don't remember the funeral, which was at St Margaret's, Westminster, where my Uncle Laurence's memorial service had been held. My father's death shut out everything but the devastating sense of loss and the loneliness it brought.

New beginnings

When I went back to school I took with me a little book that somehow had emerged in the move to Cumberland Terrace. It was a little missal that had belonged to my godfather, Henry Kemble: it became part of my life for a few years and was then mislaid. In the spring term candidates were prepared for confirmation and it was thought proper that I should be one of them. The school chaplain was a Mr Molyneux, fresh from the mission field in Melanesia; he was extremely good-looking and must have been a High Churchman, as he stalked the school grounds in cassock and biretta. The girls all had crushes on him. So when dear Miss Lang called me in to discuss my confirmation I refused, feeling the whole performance to be very 'soppy'. Whether I explained my reason for not joining in I can't recall; I expect I just said noncommittally that I would rather not. But for the next year or so I was constantly engaged with my little missal, and became particularly fond of the 'Hail Mary' prayer. I never wanted to go over to Rome and I liked Mattins and Evensong in the Church of England; but I had missed the chance of being confirmed. I never returned to the subject – or anyhow not for another forty years.

Miss Whitelaw was headmistress of Wycombe Abbey, and she had already had cause to complain of the inadequacy of my school work. She sent for me one day and questioned me searchingly about why I was such a poor performer, and what ambitions I had for when I left school. Weeping bitterly, sitting on a bentwood chair into the legs of which mine were entwined as I fidgeted wretchedly, I managed to blurt out, 'I am supposed to go on the stage – or marry and have a large family.' Miss Whitelaw found little to reassure her in this reply. For the following two terms – and my last – she went on a world tour to Australia, and dear Miss Lewis, the Housemistress of Campbell House, took over. If I had stayed at school, and had she continued in that high office, things might have been very different for me.

But after my father's death my mother realised that unlike her I was an unrewarding scholar; in addition, the expenses of Wycombe were hard to meet. So she decided that after my sixteenth birthday, in April 1920, I had better be shepherded towards the first of my chosen aims.[14] So back I went to study with Rosina Fillipi in her

14. She and her mother moved to 28 Campden House Chambers, Sheffield Terrace, Campden Hill, in 1920, the year in which her brother Laurence married.

Chelsea cottage with its charming garden, north of the King's Road behind Peter Jones. J. B. Fagan had a lease of the Court Theatre in Sloane Square, and was embarking on a production of *A Midsummer Night's Dream*. He chose me to play Titania. Mary Gray, his wife (a singer rather than an actress), was to play Oberon, Lyall Swete one of the Grecian players, and Isabel Bateman was Hermia. There had been strong ties with the Bateman family in the Lyceum days, and, having been in his company at one time or another, they all warmly welcomed Henry Irving's granddaughter.

15. 'Miss Elizabeth Irving,' ready for the stage and the *Tatler,* 1920

16. As Titania in J. B. Fagan's production of *A Midsummer Night's Dream* at the Court Theatre, London, December 1920

The Rest of the Story

by Hugo Brunner

According to the scrapbooks about her career which Elizabeth Irving compiled, no less than sixty-nine newspaper reports heralded her professional debut. Fagan's production of *A Midsummer Night's Dream* opened at the Court Theatre, London, on 6 December 1920. Her mother was present for the first night. Elizabeth was described by *The Times* as a 'charming Titania . . . a figure of slim girlish beauty, with a good voice and a touch of the artless self-consciousness natural and pleasant in a debutante'. The *Star* exemplified the many press comments on her performance: 'There are naturally signs of immaturity in her acting, but equally signs of great promise. She has grace, charm and naturalness, and a clear delivery, speaking her lines with sweetness and a sense of poetry.' She felt frightfully nervous at the dress rehearsal. But, as she told the *Observer* at the time, 'I lost my nervousness after the first long speech. . . . That speech is very difficult. . . . But when that's over I no longer feel nervous, and just love it all.'

Twice in the following year she took on the role – that of Trilby – that had made her mother famous, first with the Old Stagers in Canterbury in August and then at the Theatre Royal, Windsor, in December with the Windsor Strollers. In February 1922 she played Margrete as a guest actress with the Oxford Univesity Dramatic Society in Ibsen's *The Pretenders* at the New Theatre. Later that year she made her only film: *Shirley*, directed by A.V. Bramble. She took the title role

(far left) 17. Dorothea Baird as Trilby, the part she created and played on tour and at the Haymarket Theatre, London, in 1895

(left) 18. Elizabeth Irving as Trilby, 1921. 'The charm and beauty of Miss Elizabeth Irving would have been of little avail . . . if she had not inherited the histrionic ability of both her mother and her father.'

opposite Clive Brook. No copy of the film has survived. In November she appeared in Ian Hay's *The Happy Ending* at the St James's Theatre. She was Amy in J. M. Barrie's *Alice Sit-by-the-Fire* at the Comedy Theatre in February 1924. Later that year she met Felix Brunner at the Maughams' house, 78 Cadogan Square. She left the professional stage. Mrs Aria, writing when Elizabeth was 17, seems to have sensed that the theatre might not be her true vocation. 'Perhaps she has a far-away vision of herself in the garb of Ophelia, but she does not talk about this while she sits on the arm of my chair in a more serious consideration of the importance of dancing, and the charms of fashion, now and again showing me glimpses of her higher ideals of life.'[15]

She herself explained much later why she left the theatre. According to Don Chapman, journalist and theatre historian, who interviewed her in 1991, 'one reason was her determination not to realise the worst fears of her wealthy in-laws. Another was her feeling that the age of the actor-manager was coming to an end,' to be replaced by a more unstable and commercially led regime. Her career was rounded off on 14 April 1925, when she celebrated her twenty-first birthday in the Garrick Club. Three years later she was to make her very last appearance among professional actors. She was one of the contributors to the BBC's eightieth birthday salute to her grandfather's famous leading lady, Ellen Terry. In an excerpt from *A Midsummer Night's Dream* she repeated, in the radio broadcast, her first professional role as Titania, and Terry's great-nephew, John Gielgud, played Oberon.[16]

After her engagement, in January 1926, she began her long service as a voluntary worker by joining the House Committee of the Elizabeth Garrett Anderson Hospital, of which Lady Hall and Lady Maugham were members.[17]

Felix was then working for Brunner, Mond, the family's alkali business. He had been educated at Cheltenham and Trinity College, Oxford, and had served in the Royal Field Artillery during the Great War.

15. Aria, op.cit.
16. Don Chapman, 'Turning Down a Free Seat,' *Oxford Mail*, 5 March 1991.
17. The minute books of the committee are in the London Metropolitan Archives, Clerkenwell.

19. Portrait of Elizabeth, commissioned by Ideal Films Ltd, when making *Shirley,* a film based on Charlotte Brontë's novel

(below) 20. Wedding, July 1926. Arriving at St Margaret's, Westminster, with her brother

(below right) 21. Felix Brunner arrives for the wedding

22. With their son John at Barnabas's christening in 1932

23. Portrait in oils by R. G. Eves, c.1934. 'I have stood in front of Elizabeth Brunner's portrait in Denman College many times and given a silent thank-you to this amazing woman.' (Lynda Kiss, *The Times,* 7 February 2003)

24. The ascent of the Allalinhorn, Switzerland, in July 1937

25. Early days at Greys, with Cooleen, the labrador, and Sophie

26. With Barnabas, Dan and Hugo – round a musical box, c.1938

Felix and Elizabeth were married on 8 July 1926 in St Margaret's Church, Westminster. They honeymooned in Zermatt and Arolla in the Swiss Alps, in which Felix had climbed since he was an undergraduate. By then, Felix had begun his political career: he contested the Hulme division of Manchester, as a Liberal, in the 1924 election. Later in 1926 Brunner, Mond merged with three other companies to form ICI. The Brunner interest in the new business was immediately sold and the proceeds were placed in the Brunner Investment Trust, a company which is still quoted on the London Stock Exchange. Felix was appointed a director of the trust and later its chairman. He became a non-executive director of several other businesses and a trustee of various charities.

Their first home was at Ilchester Place. Two children were born there: John in 1927 and Nicholas in 1929, the year in which Felix contested Chippenham in a General Election. Nicholas died of meningitis in 1931. Barnabas (1932), Dan (1933) and Hugo (1935) were all born at 49 Wilton Crescent, Belgravia. In the summer of 1937 Felix and Elizabeth bought Greys Court in Oxfordshire, after briefly owning Rudloe Manor, Box, in Wiltshire and The Bill House, Selsey, Sussex. Greys was to be their home for the rest of their lives.

Elizabeth took charge of the household, the garden and the farm – with a little help of course. For the children she had had the support since 1930 of Lucienne Golaz ('Len'), who came from Nyon near Geneva. Len was not happy about living in the country and was soon replaced as nanny by 17-year-old Violet Bentley, who stayed until she began her nursing training in 1941. After that she returned to Greys when on leave and, like Len, remained a close family friend. Apart from other domestic staff, there were two gardeners, Charles Taylor and Alf May, a chauffeur, Gilbert Atkins, and a woodman, Arthur Groves. The farm was run by an adviser, Mr Palmer, but Elizabeth worked closely with him and took a keen interest in the herd of pedigree Guernseys. She herself used to make butter, while often expecting her sons to do the churning. In 1954 she was president of the Henley and District Agricultural Association and welcomed the annual show to Greys that July.

On arrival at Rotherfield Greys, Elizabeth joined the village

Women's Institute. In the autumn of 1939, she played her part in the movement's response to Government's plea for help with city children fleeing the blitz; she welcomed to Greys Court two families of evacuees from west London, the Bentons and the Campions. In 1941 she became chairman of the Oxfordshire Federation. Later in the war she was appointed to the National Executive. Soon after it she became a magistrate and sat on the Henley bench until she retired from it in 1974. Her national presence in the WIs led to her becoming a member of the sub-committee set up 'to explore the idea of a WI Conference House'. Barbara Kaye, the first historian of Denman College, wrote that 'it was largely due to her drive and determination to overcome all obstacles that the idea became a reality' in 1948 in the manor house at Marcham, then in Berkshire now in Oxfordshire.[18] She twice served as president of the Oxfordshire WI in the late forties and then as national chairman from 1951 to 1956. She followed that by leading its National Drama Festival in 1957: five plays on the lives of poets were commissioned, and she and her son Barnabas played in Robert Gittings' one, about William Cowper. During her chairmanship the movement was instrumental in the founding of the national campaigning charity, the Keep Britain Tidy Group. She was its first chairman and from 1966 its president. 'For devotion to the work of the group and for her continual concern for its success since its inception' she was appointed OBE in 1964. By that time she had also become chairman of the Women's Group on Public Welfare, founded by Margaret Bondfield in 1939. The historian of the National Council of Social Service wrote that Elizabeth 'was the inspiration of many of the achievements of these years', the sixties.[19] She was a member of the General Advisory Group of the BBC from 1968 to 1971.

In 1969, Elizabeth and Felix gave Greys Court to the National Trust. Over the years she had made many changes both to the house and the gardens. Soon after they arrived she invited Gertrude Knoblock to make the four statues that adorn the curtain wall beside

18. *The Story of Denman College 1948–1969,* London, 1970.

19. Margaret E. Brasnett, *Voluntary Social Action: A History of the National Council of Social Service 1919–1969,* London 1970.

27. The president, with supporters, at the Annual General Meeting of the Oxfordshire Federation of Women's Institutes, Rhodes House, Oxford, 1947. *Left to right:* Helena Deneke; Miss E. Sandars, county secretary; Elizabeth; Margaret Deneke; Elsie Corbett, of Spelsbury, local historian. The Deneke sisters were great figures in the life of Lady Margaret Hall and of what is now the Oxford Chamber Music Society.

28. She spoke the prologue and epilogue in the Festival of Britain Pageant performed at Blenheim Palace in the summer of 1951. The pageant, written by John Masefield, was put on by the Oxfordshire Federation of Women's Institutes and the Oxfordshire Rural Community Council.

29. With Betty Christmas, Warden of Denman College, celebrating the fifth birthday of the college in 1953

30. Addressing the AGM of the National Federation of Women's Institutes in June 1953. She was chairman from 1951 to 1956.

the house. The main changes to the house itself were the demolition of the Victorian service buildings and ballroom during the war and the addition, in the 1980s, of a garden room, designed by Francis Pollen and decorated by Richard Shirley Smith. The mark she made on the gardens was impressive. Her innovations included the White Garden below the main mediaeval tower (the Great Tower); its kidney-shaped pond was made by her son John and the loggia, designed by Ptolemy Dean, was her last gift to the National Trust. She invited Francis Pollen to build a Chinese bridge in honour of a close family friend, Yan-kit So (completed in 1979), and a maze to honour another friend, Archbishop Robert Runcie, who came to Greys to dedicate it in October 1981. Pollen also designed a stone tank, with a fountain at its centre, for her. Her many new plantings were complemented by stone carvings and furniture which she delighted in commissioning. All this, of course, cost money and she often acknowledged that her marriage to Felix made possible this kind of expenditure, as well as her generosity to many people. The spirit in which they undertook such projects was expressed by Elizabeth in conversation with Mary Keen: 'places like this have to be shared.'[20]

The gardens were the scene of many events in which she was deeply involved: family parties, village fêtes, pageants, plays, musical evenings and, most notably, a *son et lumière* drama, which Christopher Ede produced in 1959 and 1961. For this she commissioned Robert Gittings to write a play, with Greys associations, about the murder of Sir Thomas Overbury in 1613. Music for it was composed by the pianist Denis Matthews.

Elizabeth loved the garden, and she enjoyed making patchwork quilts and jam, and cooking. Reading meant a great deal to her: she had a particular devotion to the novels of Charlotte M. Yonge but she was generally well read in the Victorian novelists and in biography, new and old. Many have avowed that she had a great gift for friendship, expressed in hospitality and in numerous lively letters. Her close friends included a Swiss cousin of Felix, Rico Steinbrüchel, who came into their lives when he visited London in 1948 to work with

20. 'A Spirit of Place', *Perspectives,* August 1995.

31. Buttoning up the waistcoat given to the actor Kenneth More after he opened the Greys fete in 1955

32. The wedding of Rico and Hanni Steinbrüchel, Zürich, November 1964

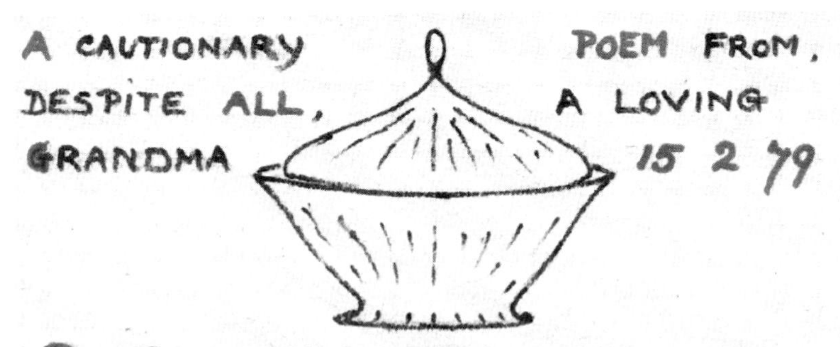

A CAUTIONARY POEM FROM, DESPITE ALL, A LOVING GRANDMA 15 2 79

ON GRANDMA'S DRESSER USED TO STAND
AN OBJECT THAT MUST NOW BE BANNED
FROM GREEDY CHILDREN, SEEKING FOR
THE SUGAR LUMPS THAT THEY ADORE!
WITHIN THE BOWL, LAST SUNDAY, WERE
FULL FORTY LUMPS A-LYING THERE –
BUT THEN A BAND OF TINY TOTS
TOOK ONE – OR TWO – OR THREE – THEN LOTS
AND BY THE TIME THEY WENT AWAY
GRANDMA REGARDED WITH DISMAY
AN EMPTY SUGAR BOWL! ALACK!
THAT SUCH A NAUGHTY LITTLE PACK
OF GREEDY GUTS SHOULD COME TO CALL
AND THUS ON GRANDMA'S SUGAR FALL!
THIS UNWISE GUZZLING WILL BEQUEATH
A LEGACY OF ACHING TEETH!
SO CHILDREN DEAR, I BEG OF YOU
SUCH SELF INDULGENCE TO ESCHEW!

33. Sugar poem, 1979 – a gift for light verse, which both Laurence and Elizabeth inherited from their father.

34. Felix and Elizabeth in old age, 1982, a painting by Bill Mundy

35. 'The Old Gardener' by Jacqueline Geldart, one of many works she commissioned for the garden at Greys

36. As vice-president of Keep Britain Tidy at the launch of the Beautiful Britain Campaign in May 1988 in Westminster Hall, London, with the Duke of Edinburgh, Lord Ezra (president of Keep Britain Tidy), and Lord Parry of Neyland (chairman)

a London law firm. Rico made several holiday journeys with them before he got married; later he and his wife, Hanni, joined them for many years in August at the Hotel Bella Tola et St Luc in the Val d'Anniviers in the Valais. She loved and admired Switzerland, its people and its mountains – she and Felix climbed the Allalinhorn (4027 metres) in 1937. Neither Sir Henry Irving, whose memory she revered, nor Switzerland were to be spoken ill of in her company.

The importance to her of the WI can't be exaggerated. Helen Carey, another national chairman writing in the *Independent* after her death, described it as 'her lasting passion and joy . . . Of particular interest to her was the cultural life of a community which, she believed, contributed to spiritual well-being. She actively promoted and made available art, music and drama to a wider audience through membership of the WI.'[21] She herself once said, 'I can't think how you would live in a village if you didn't belong to the WI.' The movement appealed to her as a milieu in which women could flourish but which was not hostile to men. And it was one in which her skills as an actress could be confidently deployed: a large audience of women at the Royal Albert Hall had no fears for someone who had performed before 1500 soldiers. It was a world too in which her gaiety, her enjoyment of life and her sense of fun were appreciated.

Felix and Elizabeth celebrated their golden wedding at Greys Court in 1976. He died in 1982. She celebrated her eightieth birthday in the hall in Trinity College, Oxford, where three of her sons, following their father, had been undergraduates. There was a party for her ninetieth birthday in a marquee on the top lawn at Greys. That day she received a telemessage from The Queen Mother, first patron of Keep Britain Tidy, and an electric buggy from the family, to enable her to continue to enjoy the garden. Her last years confined her more and more to Greys, though she continued to visit Baden in Switzerland in winter until her nineties and made her last visit to St Luc in 2001. She gained great satisfaction from talking to people who visited the house and gardens, and by whom she could often be seen making jam in the kitchen. She died on 9 January

21. The *Independent*, 15 January 2010.

37. In front of J. W. H. Bartlett's portrait of her grandfather, Sir Henry Irving, in the School Room at Greys in 1991

38. With her eldest son, John, and his daughter, Claire, in the Antico restaurant, Henley-on-Thames. It was in this restaurant that 'she delighted in setting fire to Amaretto wrappers and seeing their disintegrating ash falling on to someone else's table.'

2003, at the age of 98. Her funeral was in Greys church, to which she and Felix had contributed a new east window, and she was buried in the churchyard there beside Felix. A memorial service was held in April in the parish church in Henley. The Marchioness of Anglesey (her old friend and successor as chairman of the NFWI), Jean-Jacques Steinbrüchel (reading an address written by his uncle Rico), and one of her granddaughters, Isabel Sharp, spoke at it. The service was followed by a party in a marquee on the front lawn at Greys. In 2009 she was noticed as a 'voluntary worker', in an article written by Shirley Anglesey in the *Oxford Dictionary of National Biography*.

Elizabeth was widely loved and admired. Her dear friend and WI colleague, Nancy Tennant, considered that Lady Denman, first chairman of the movement, 'was immensely respected, but she was not loved in the way that Elizabeth Brunner was loved, as a person, as a very warm person'.[22] But she could also be seen as formidable, especially by her grandchildren. Nevertheless, as one of them, Isabel, said at her memorial service, she would have seemed 'an alarming figure, had it not been that she allowed of a kind of fellow feeling with the young and the small, a tenderness and empathy which must have been based on her own vulnerability'.

Like her mother, Elizabeth had mixed feelings about the theatre, but it was in her blood and she often talked of the theatre of her youth and its people, some of whom, like Richard Goolden and Miles Malleson, she had played with and later took her children to see. But her greatest theatre friend was the playwright Ben Travers. Ben's wife, Violet, and her own mother had been the only women in the audience when she started her career at the Savoy theatre in 1916. In his first volume of autobiography, *Vale of Laughter*, he wrote: 'Elizabeth has always presented a problem. Is she more beautiful in looks than she is kind at heart or the other way about? I think the only solution is that it's a dead heat.'[23] She laughed at that, but it must have pleased her very much.

22. Quoted in Anne Stamper, *Rooms off the Corridor: Education in the WI and 50 years of Denman College 1948–1998*, London, 1998. Elizabeth wrote about Lady Denman for the *Dictionary of National Biography 1951–60*, Oxford, 1980.
23. *Vale of Laughter: an Autobiography*, London, 1957.

39. In front of the house for an interview with the local paper, 1994

40. In the Anniversary Walk on the buggy which her children gave her for her ninetieth birthday, in April 1994

41. Outside Denman College in 1997 with Anne Stamper, author of *Rooms off the Corridor,* the book celebrating its fiftieth anniversary